I0189795

IMAGES
of America

MADISON AND
HAMILTON

BRIDGE BOUCKVILLE NY

ON THE COVER: The Landmark Tavern was also known as the Cobblestone Store, Old Stone Store, and the Coe & Brockett Store. It was built in 1850 by James Coolidge, a New Englander who started the first hops in the area in 1808. The Landmark is a one-of-a-kind building in the country. Hidden spaces behind fireplaces, which are now filled in, are believed to have been used to conceal runaway slaves on their way to freedom. The cupola had six sides: one for each of the owner's wives. All of his wives, including the sixth wife-to-be, died before the building was finished. (Author's collection.)

IMAGES
of America

MADISON AND HAMILTON

Mishell Kyle Forward-Magnusson

ARCADIA
PUBLISHING

Copyright © 2012 by Mishell Kyle Forward-Magnusson
ISBN 978-1-5316-5082-7

Published by Arcadia Publishing
Charleston, South Carolina

Library of Congress Control Number: 2011934175

For all general information, please contact Arcadia Publishing:
Telephone 843-853-2070
Fax 843-853-0044
E-mail sales@arcadiapublishing.com
For customer service and orders:
Toll-Free 1-888-313-2665

Visit us on the Internet at www.arcadiapublishing.com

This book has been created in large part due to contributions from my father, Fay Harold Forward. I learned during this project that at his age he has a fantastic memory of what took place in the Towns of Madison and Hamilton. This book is dedicated with love to my dad.

CONTENTS

ACKNOWLEDGMENTS

The first person to thank is my husband, Michael, who has always encouraged and supported what I do! I also wish to acknowledge my brothers, Jeff C. Forward and Justin F. Forward. It is Jeff's fault that I undertook this project, as he started giving me Arcadia books 10 years ago and continues to every Christmas. Justin seems just as interested as I am with what parts of our area today are made up from what came from yesterday.

In addition, special thanks go to both Jim Ford and John Taibi. Jim piqued my interest in local history way back in the seventh grade and continues to today through books he put together about local history. John brought the local history of railroading to my attention in his fascinating way of bringing the past to the present. Thank you goes to Diane VanSlyke for all those trips to Madison!

The pictures in this book come from several sources, many from mine, Jim Ford's, and John Taibi's collections. In addition, pictures were received from the Town of Madison Historical Society, the Chenango Canal Association, Glenn and Judi Forward, Gary Fuess, *Limestone Locks and Overgrowth* by Michele A. McFee, Ron and Viola Neff, and the Madison County Historical Society. Unless otherwise stated, all photographs are from my collection.

Thank you to all of these sources for their willingness to share.

INTRODUCTION

The Towns of Madison and Hamilton are located in what is now Madison County. The County of Madison is found just about in the center of New York State. Counties were first established in New York state in 1683. At that time, what is now Madison County was actually part of Albany County, which spanned a large part of the state. The first change in the size of Albany County occurred in 1766 with the creation of Cumberland County; Albany County was reduced again in 1770 and again in 1772, 1783, 1789, 1791, 1798, and once more in March 19, 1806, when the New York State Senate gave us the current configuration.

The geographic center of New York State is located at Pratts Hollow in the town of Eaton in Madison County. Madison County is made up of 14 towns, including Brookfield, Cazenovia, DeRuyter, Eaton, Fenner, Georgetown, Hamilton, Lebanon, Lenox, Lincoln, Madison, Nelson, Smithfield, and Sullivan, and one city, Oneida. This book is intended to cover the towns of Madison and Hamilton. Hamilton is a town with a population of approximately 5,700 people according to the 2010 census. The town is named after American patriot Alexander Hamilton. The town of Hamilton contains a village also named Hamilton, which is the site of Colgate University. The village is on the county's border. The location was formerly called Payne's Corners. The town of Hamilton was established in 1795, prior to the formation of the county, from the town of Paris in Oneida County. The original town was reduced to create new towns in the county. When the original town of Hamilton was reduced, one of the towns created was Madison, with an estimated population of 2,800 as of the 2010 census.

Communities located within the town of Hamilton include Beekman Corners, which is a location between Hamilton Village and East Hamilton; Brooks Corners, a hamlet in the south part of the town on Route 12; Darts Corners, located between the village of Hamilton and East Hamilton; the village of Earlville; East Hamilton, a hamlet on Route 12, east of the village; Excell Corners, located northeast of South Hamilton; and Hamilton Center, a hamlet southeast of the village. The town of Hamilton also includes Hubbardsville, Loomis Corners, Poolville, Shores Corners, and South Hamilton.

The town of Madison lies on the east border of the county, south of center. It is bounded on the north by Stockbridge and Augusta, east by Sangerfield and Brookfield, south by Hamilton, and west by Eaton and totals 22,500 acres.

Its principal stream is the Oriskany Creek. Also, a branch of the Chenango River is Payne Creek, which feeds Lake Moraine; Lake Moraine has 235 acres and has a feeder canal two miles long to the Chenango Canal.

The town has 3.5 miles of summit-level canal within its boundary that are still controlled by the state.

The Ontario & Western Railroad, which is abandoned, crossed the town and was contiguous to the canal.

Solsville on the Oriskany Creek was the location of sawmills and gristmills. One mill bore the names of Dalrymple's Sawmill, Howard's Mill, and, later, Solsville in honor of Solomon Alcott, a resident and manufacturer of potash.

The Solsville gristmill was built around 1810 by Gen. Erastus Cleaveland, who was succeeded in ownership by his son-in-law Nathan Niles Howard. During the latter's occupancy, it stood idle some 18 years pending Howard's efforts to obtain remuneration from the state for damages sustained by the opening of the canal. He received some $10,000 by three different appraisements. On Howard's death, January 21, 1855, the property passed to his brother Adin, who transferred it soon after to A.C. Wheeler, who refitted it, put in new machinery, and operated it for a few years. Wheeler sold it to William A. Simmons, who, after two or three years, sold to William S. Pierce, who sold to James H. Parker.

The construction of the Cherry Valley Turnpike (present-day Route 20) in 1803 was one of the most pivotal events in the town of Madison's history. The turnpike brought trade from the east and a constant stream of settlers heading west.

The town of Madison contains a village also named Madison; Bouckville, a hamlet near the west town line on Route 20; Durfee Corners, a location in the southeastern part of the town; Lake Moraine, a lake south of Madison Village; Madison Center, a hamlet also south of the village; and Sigby Corners and Solsville, both hamlets.

The hamlet of Bouckville holds many significant historical distinctions, like the summit of the Chenango Canal, a well-known baseball team, the original home of Mott's Apple Company, and its most renowned claim as the original place that hops were first grown commercially in the United States and where James Coolidge settled.

Madison is well known because of the Madison Wind Farm, built in 2000, and the Madison/Bouckville Antique Festival, which draws over 60,000 people a year.

One

HOP INDUSTRY

The following is a superb description of the time from James Fenimore Cooper:

> Those were the days when the "hop was king," and the whole countryside was one great hop yard, and beautiful. It was the hop that built many of the big farm houses, now abandoned. Many a farmer made the value of his farm out of a single good year's crop. When the time came for harvesting the crop, the air of the town became tense; the housewives became worried as all the help insisted on a week off to go "hop pickin'." There were rumors of great camps of tramps in the woods about to raid the town; the police force of two men, one with one arm and the other with one leg, became worried and patrolled the town until one a.m. instead of the quitting at eleven p.m. as was customary. No one went abroad after dark unless armed with a pistol, more dangerous to the owner than to his enemy. They were the halcyon days for the boys and young men who tip-toed about the town looking for the invaders and listening to the tales of the police patrol, one with a club and one with a lantern. The street lamps burned until twelve instead of being turned out at eleven, and the whole atmosphere was one of suppressed alarm and excitement. Thousands of tough "pickers" came from the cities to earn the eighty cents a box for pickin', and to enjoy the nightly barn dances given for their amusement.

The details of this time in the towns of Madison County are included in *Tinged With Gold: Hop Culture in the United States*, by Michael A. Tomlan.

Throughout the 19th and 20th centuries, hop growing in Madison County was an important agricultural industry. Hops not only brought prosperity to the farmers who engaged in this business but also brought a unique way of life to the people of Madison County.

James D. Coolidge first introduced growing hops on a commercial level to Madison County in 1808. Coolidge purchased a farm near Bouckville in the town of Madison. Since hops were already being grown on a small noncommercial scale in Madison, Coolidge was able to buy a number of hop roots from his neighbors to start his own hop yard.

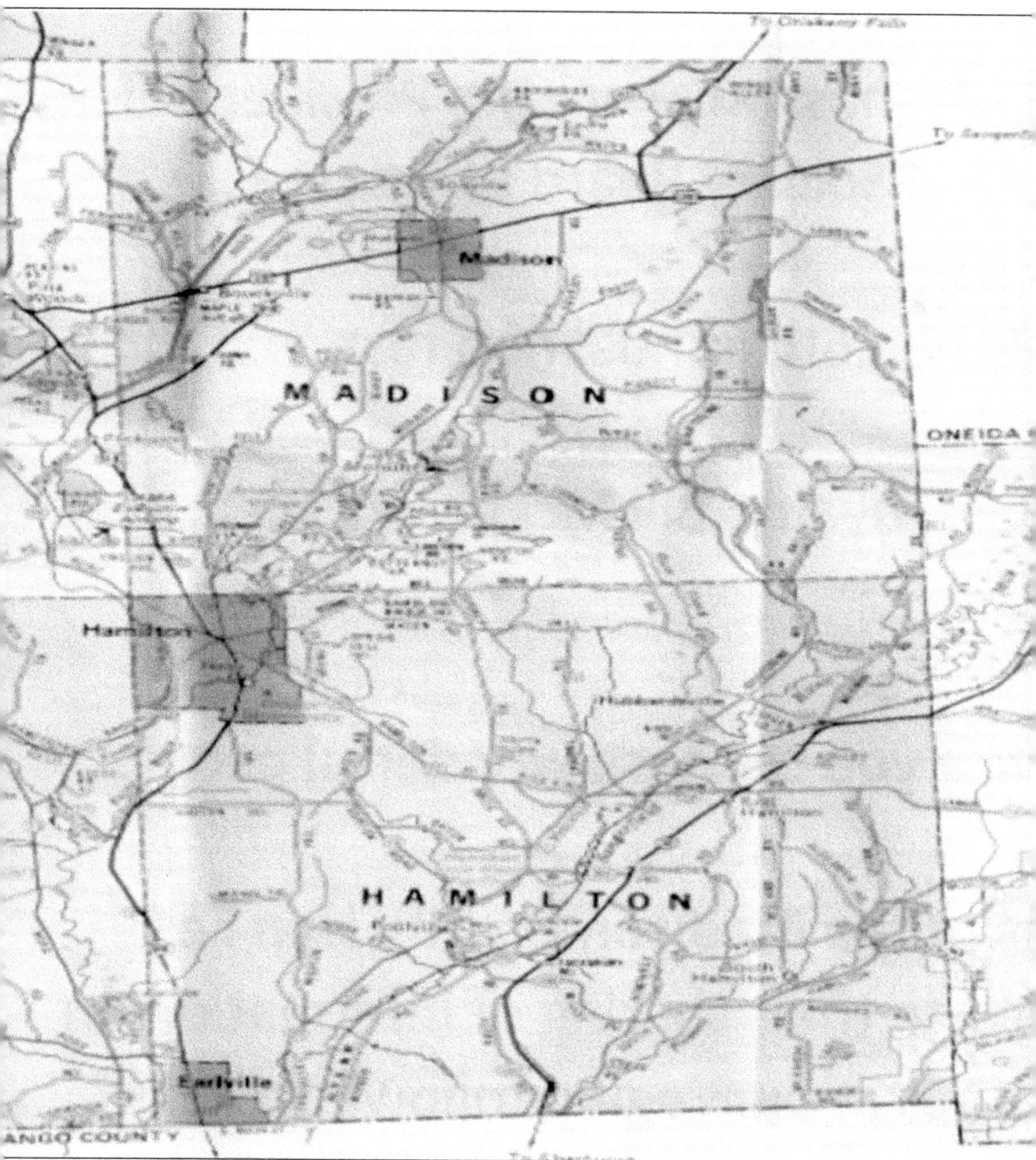

This section of a map shows the towns of Hamilton and Madison, Hamilton being to the south of Madison. The map indicates where the "old" canal went through as well as where the villages of Hamilton and Madison are located within the towns. In addition, this map is intended to give the reader a reference to the lakes and other hamlets that are mentioned throughout the material.

This is James Coolidge's original house, which was located on what is now Route 12B in the town of Madison and became the Ford farm for many years. James Coolidge brought hops to Madison County, making the town of Madison the largest commercial crop grower in the country at the time. (Courtesy of Ron and Viola Neff.)

This is the Coolidge oast house, with the frame kiln that was added later, near Bouckville around 1850. The cobblestone kiln with attendant frame barn was mistakenly believed to be the earliest kiln in the region due to being one of the most visible ones located on Route 20. It was razed in the 1970s.

Hop pickers were usually women, but some men also picked hops. Hop boxes were divided into four compartments, with one picker for each compartment. In this picture are, from left to right, Allie White, an unidentified man, Edna Coe, Maude Anguish, Mabel Davis, and Rose Livermore. (Courtesy of the Town of Madison Historical Society.)

Picking in 1902, Josephine Palmeter is the third woman from the right, and Zella Palmeter is second from the right. The average hop picker picked two boxes of hops a day, but a fast picker could pick four or five. When a box was full, the picker yelled "Hop sack," and the pole puller or yard foreman came over and emptied the hops into a sack. (Courtesy of the Town of Madison Historical Society.)

Developing a hop business required great expense. The materials required to plant and grow hop plants ranged from hop rhizomes to hop poles. The stem of the plant is a bine. A bine twines itself, whereas a vine has tendrils that attach the stem to a pole as it grows. The hop bine follows the sun around a pole.

This aerial of Bouckville from Stowell's Hill looking towards Crow Hill shows fields of poles in the storage position. To the grower, the most important reason for raising hops was to make a significant amount of money in a short amount of time. Many farmers made the value of their farms out of a single good year's crop. (Courtesy Helen Nower.)

This hop kiln was located on what was known as the Washburn Farm, which became Harold Forward's on Crow Hill in Bouckville. The drying kiln is in the middle with the four-sided roof. This picture shows the proud horses used to run the farm in the 1930s. The kiln was gone by the 1940s, and the end of the barn was opened by the 1950s. (Courtesy Glenn and Judi Forward.)

This group of seven men has stopped to pose for the camera in the middle of the hop field with poles and bines all around them. The bine can grow as much as 12 inches a day in June and will grow 20–30 feet in one season after it is established. Hops are primarily used for flavoring malt liquors, such as beer and ale. Over 90 percent of these hops were sold locally.

This is a great picture of the hops bine growing up the pole. Hops were also used for making medicine and tea. A popular medicine in the 19th century was hop bitters, which claimed to cure dyspepsia, urinary disease, kidney disease, nervousness, indigestion, liver complaints, and general debility. (Courtesy of the Town of Madison Historical Society.)

This is the last known hop kiln with a weather vane in the area. Once picked, hops needed to be dried fairly quickly. At least once a day, a wagon came along and picked up the bags of hops to take to the kiln. (Courtesy of Madison County Historical Society.)

This is a drying room within the kiln. The first floor contained the stove for heating the kiln and the press room for bailing the hops. The second floor was used for drying and storing the hops. Note its slatted floor. Once the hops were dried, they were formed into bails to be taken to market. (Courtesy of Madison County Historical Society.)

This photograph is a good illustration of the workings of a hop field. Stripped of hop bines, stacked poles can be seen on the left. Teams of wagons, visible in the center, hauled poles to and from pickers, stacked poles, and transported bags of hops to the kiln. In the background, pickers work at hop boxes. The standing poles in the distance attest to the amount of work yet to be done.

The Landmark Tavern, known as the Old Stone Store at the time of this photograph, was built by the Coolidge family between 1849 and 1851. Lewis T. Coe and H.D. Brockett bought the building in 1886. After Coe died, Brockett sold it to Charles M. Coe, the son of Lewis.

Coolidge's building is an outstanding example of cobblestone construction and is associated with the development of Bouckville as an important center of hop culture in Madison County. This picture was taken just after electricity came to the area. In 2000, Ye Olde Landmark Tavern (as it is now known) was placed in National Register of Historic Places.

Two

CHENANGO CANAL

In Central New York during the first half of the 19th century, the canals were the mainstay of the manufacturing centers. The Erie Canal connected the Hudson River with Lake Erie, and between those two points made it possible for places like Utica, Rome, and Syracuse to become important producers of manufactured goods. The Chenango Canal followed the course of the Chenango River and Oriskany Creek—the origin of Oriskany being in Bouckville. During this time period, Binghamton was the most important municipality in the southern tier of the state, because it was located on the mighty Susquehanna River at the junction of the Chenango River. The building of the Chenango Canal between Binghamton and Utica meant not only creating an improved transportation thoroughfare but also, and more importantly, connecting two early centers of commerce.

New York State spent a large amount of money to build the Chenango Canal. When completed in October 1836, the 97-mile-long canal had cost $2,782,124. The problem with this was that, even at this early date, there were some in the state government who foresaw the coming of the railroads. They knew that the railroads would eventually eclipse the canals in importance.

The village green in Hamilton might still be a swamp today if the Chenango Canal had not come through. The local engineer for the waterway suggested that the dirt excavated from the canal bed be used to fill in the swampy area. Ferdinand Walker, whose store was on the west side of Broad Street, liked the idea and raised subscriptions to pay for it.

Before the canal was constructed there was a tavern at McClure's Settlement, as Bouckville was known then, but no post office. The town's location on the Cherry Valley turnpike fostered its growth early on. In 1824, some of the leading men in the area changed the name of the settlement to Johnsville. When the canal came through and a post office was to be established, another name had to be chosen, because there were a number of other towns named Johnsville in the state.

In *Limestone Locks and Overgrowth*, Michele A. McFee states, "Competition from the railroads, the cost of upkeep, political pressure, the enlargement of the Erie Canal and other factors loosened the waterway's already tenuous hold on the Chenango Canal."

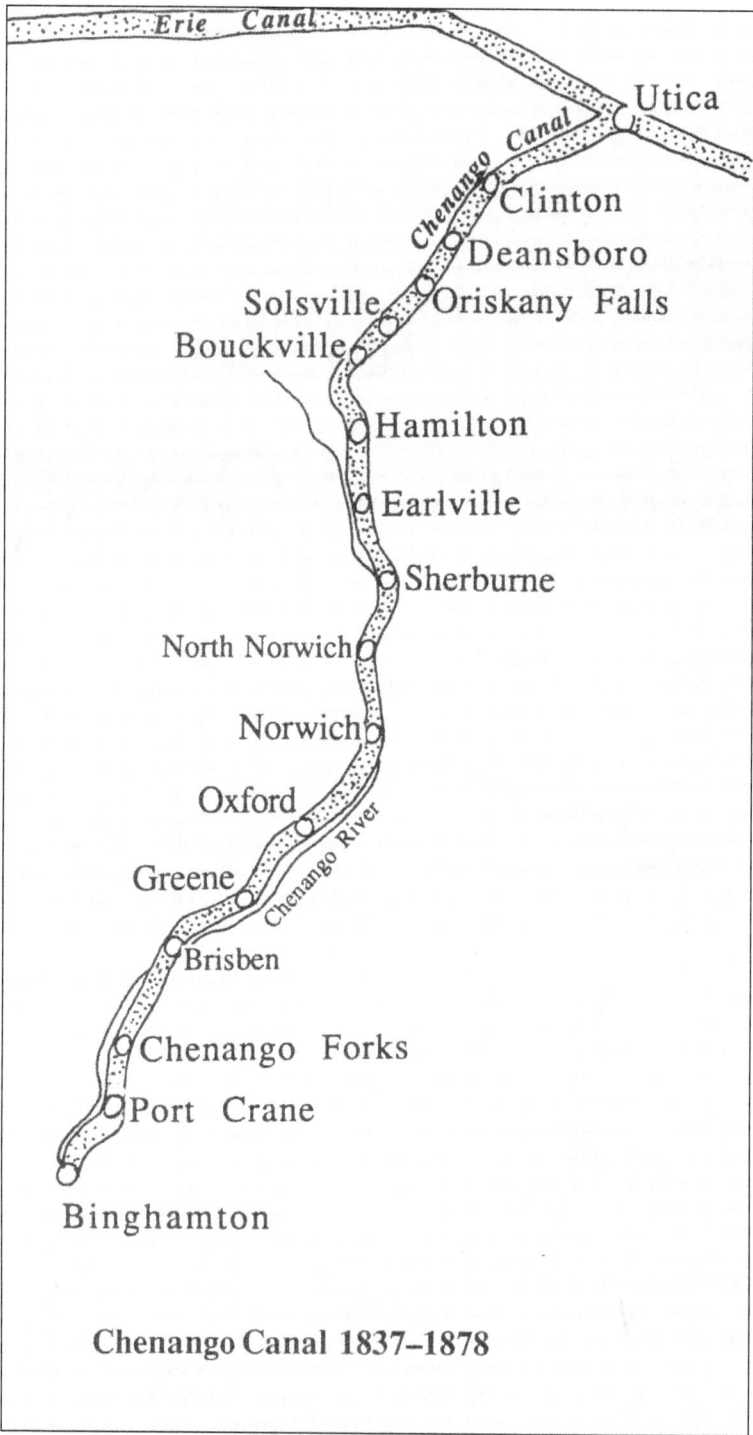

Erie Canal

Utica

Chenango Canal

Clinton

Deansboro

Solsville / **Oriskany Falls**

Bouckville

Hamilton

Earlville

Sherburne

North Norwich

Norwich

Oxford

Chenango River

Greene

Brisben

Chenango Forks

Port Crane

Binghamton

Chenango Canal 1837–1878

This map illustrates the entire span of the Chenango Canal from Utica to Binghamton, which was in operation from 1837 to 1878. Bouckville is known as the summit because it is the highest point along the entire route. From Bouckville, the canal goes "down" to Utica to the north and "down" to Binghamton to the south. (Courtesy of Michele A. McFee.)

Old Chenango Canal. Bouckville N Y.

This is the original bridge at Bouckville that carried Route 20 over the canal; the bridge was built on Squire Whipple's design. This is what was called a "bowstring truss" design and was patented in 1841. Whipple, an Erie Canal surveyor and then an engineer for the New York State & Erie Railroad, was an important force in truss-building technology.

CANAL & BRIDGE
BOUCKVILLE.N y

This is a view farther back of the Squire Whipple design, which served as both an arch and a truss. It was characterized by a top chord that stretched like a bow, meeting each end of the bridge at the abutments; between the bow and the bottom chord were vertical and diagonal pieces.

This picture shows the cider mills along both sides of the canal well after the close of the canal, with no more boats going yonder. The building going over the bridge in this photograph was not there when the canal was in operation. The buildings along the east side of the canal were not replaced after the last fire. (Courtesy of the Chenango Canal Association.)

In 1925, the Cherry Valley Turnpike Bridge going over the canal collapsed. In this photograph, there is a car in the remains of the bridge. Thankfully no one was hurt. There is no doubt that the man driving the car had no idea what to do. Many people from miles around came to see the results.

This picture shows the folks who came from miles around to observe the wreckage of the collapse of the bridge over the Chenango Canal in Bouckville in 1925. These folks are looking at the view from the other side of the canal, where there was a fence conveniently located (as compared to the previous picture) to tell the story many times over.

This picture depicts the canal during a quiet time. Bouckville was located between Lock No. 76 just south of Solsville and Lock No. 77 just north of Hamilton and was the largest village on the summit level of the canal. The canal bed was in a deep cut as it went through Bouckville. (Courtesy of the Chenango Canal Association.)

Jenny Fairchild, on a bridge, shows her house across the canal. The picture had to be taken after 1876 when the canal closed, as no bridge went over the canal like this when it was in operation. A boat could not get under this bridge. Fairchild looks to be in her Sunday best. (Courtesy of the Chenango Canal Association.)

There was a wealthy farming community around Solsville that benefited immensely when the canal came through town. Farm products were loaded onto boats in the village, and there was a general store where area residents could buy supplies that came in on the canal. (Courtesy of the Town of Madison Historical Society.)

This photograph was taken from the Edgarton farm, which was located between Solsville and Bouckville, looking south toward Bouckville. This is after the canal closed, as the towpath is overgrown. Many houses along the canal were built with stones brought from quarries along the canal by boat. (Courtesy of Gary Fuess.)

This photograph from 1957 shows the remains of the farm bridge on the Edgarton farm. The wood planks that covered the bridge surface are seen on the left of the picture, and the "safety" handrail is still across the span. Albert Edgarton is seen driving the team of horses back up the hill after the horses drank in the canal. (Courtesy of Gary Fuess.)

In 1926, these three girls are cooling off in the canal at the Smith Edgarton farm, later owned by Albert Edgarton. Pictured on the left is Ruth Edgarton Reynolds, later Ruth Edgarton Fuess. The younger girl may be Ruth's sister. (Courtesy of Gary Fuess.)

This 1968 picture shows the waterfall area, which was the aqueduct along Canal Road, looking west toward the Livermore farm. The canal went over the Oriskany Creek, where this waterfall is located, between Solsville and Bouckville. The Oriskany Creek originates in the hills in this area. (Courtesy of the Chenango Canal Association.)

This is a close up look at Lock No. 68 between Bouckville and Solsville taken in 1968, ninety years after the canal closed. This shows how well the canal locks were made and what engineering techniques there were in the 19th century. Very few of the stones have come out. (Courtesy of the Chenango Canal Association.)

Here is a picture of Lock No. 68 between Bouckville and Solsville. This one was taken in 2009, and it is amazing how well the lock continues to hold up, comparing it to the one above, taken 41 years earlier. The people in the picture are on a Chenango Canal Association tour, with this being a very popular spot to obverse the makings of the locks of the Chenango Canal. (Courtesy of the Chenango Canal Association.)

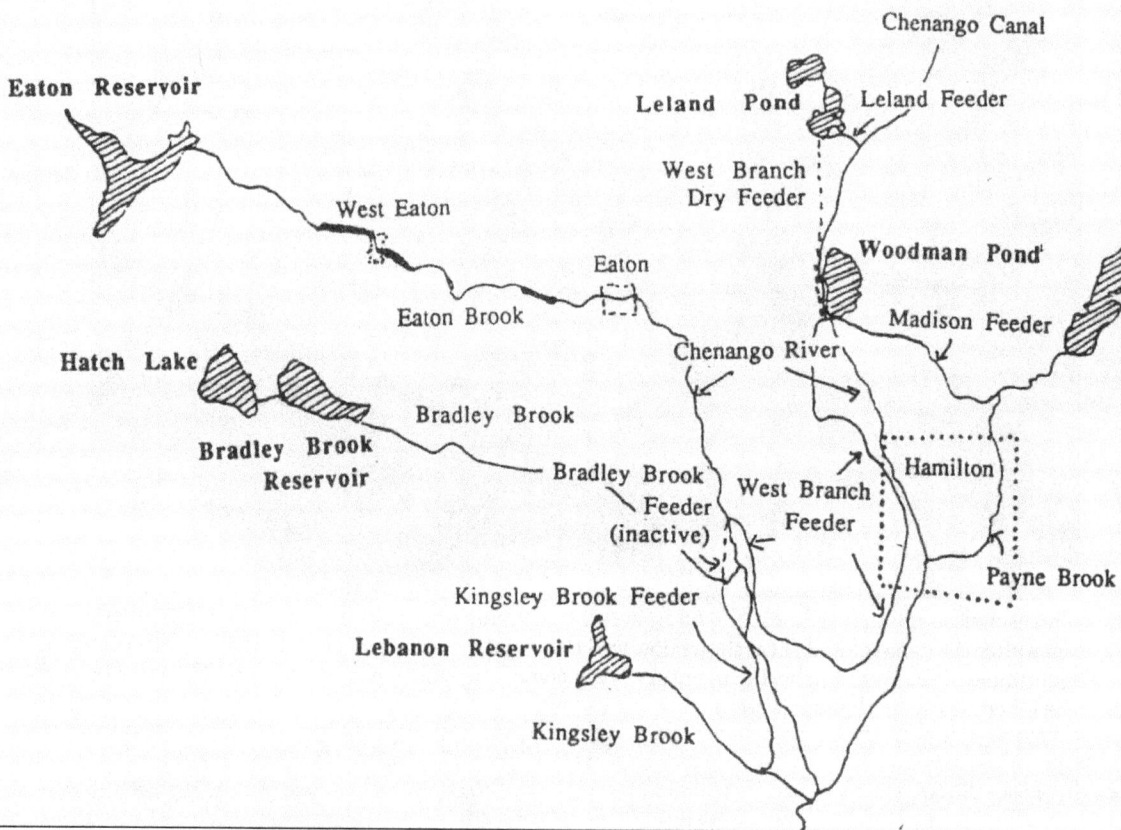

Eaton Reservoir

Chenango Canal

Leland Pond · Leland Feeder

West Branch
Dry Feeder

West Eaton

Eaton

Woodman Pond

Eaton Brook

Madison Feeder

Chenango River

Hatch Lake

Bradley Brook

Bradley Brook
Reservoir

Bradley Brook
Feeder
(inactive)

West Branch
Feeder

Hamilton

Payne Brook

Kingsley Brook Feeder

Lebanon Reservoir

Kingsley Brook

This is an illustration of the canal system and all of its feeders in the town of Hamilton area. The complicated summit-level feeder system was used to direct water to the northern section of the canal. Note the village of Hamilton in the square and the lakes depicted here. (Courtesy of Michele A. McFee.)

This photograph was taken looking north along a feeder from the New York State dam to the canal. Water from Lebanon Reservoir, Eaton Brook Reservoir, Bradley Brook Reservoir, Hopkins Reservoir, and the Chenango River flows between these banks to supply the canal to the east. (Courtesy of Madison County Historical Society.)

This is the Lebanon Reservoir control gate at the foot of the dam. This shows the use of stones and the gate to control the water, which can be let from the reservoir to feed the canal system. Still in use today, it sends water along the old Chenango Canal to the Erie Canal System. (Courtesy of Madison County Historical Society.)

Looking at the underside of an overpass, the sun shines through for a view of the canal. The Chenango Canal water supply comes from Lake Leland as well as Lake Moraine. (Courtesy of Madison County Historical Society.)

In this photograph is one of the Chenango Canal water-supply lakes. It is known as Lower Lake Leland, and pictured are its dam and gate house. Lake Leland, now known as Leland's Pond, has two areas with a road splitting the lake. (Courtesy of Madison County Historical Society.)

This is a narrow, deep channel that is about 80 feet long. This channel connects Upper Lake Leland to Lower Lake Leland. Route 26 runs through the middle of the lake, splitting what is now known as Leland's Pond into two parts, Upper Lake Leland and Lower Lake Leland. (Courtesy of Madison County Historical Society.)

STREET SCENE, BOUCKVILLE, N.Y. 20.

This is a street scene looking at that wonderful Whipple bridge that the Chenango Canal went under at the summit of the entire canal in Bouckville. The Chenango Canal let to the Erie Canal, and the Erie Canal gave Madison County farmers the ability to ship their hops easily and cheaply to eastern markets. Chenango Canal also opened up expanding western markets in Ohio, Michigan, Illinois, and Indiana.

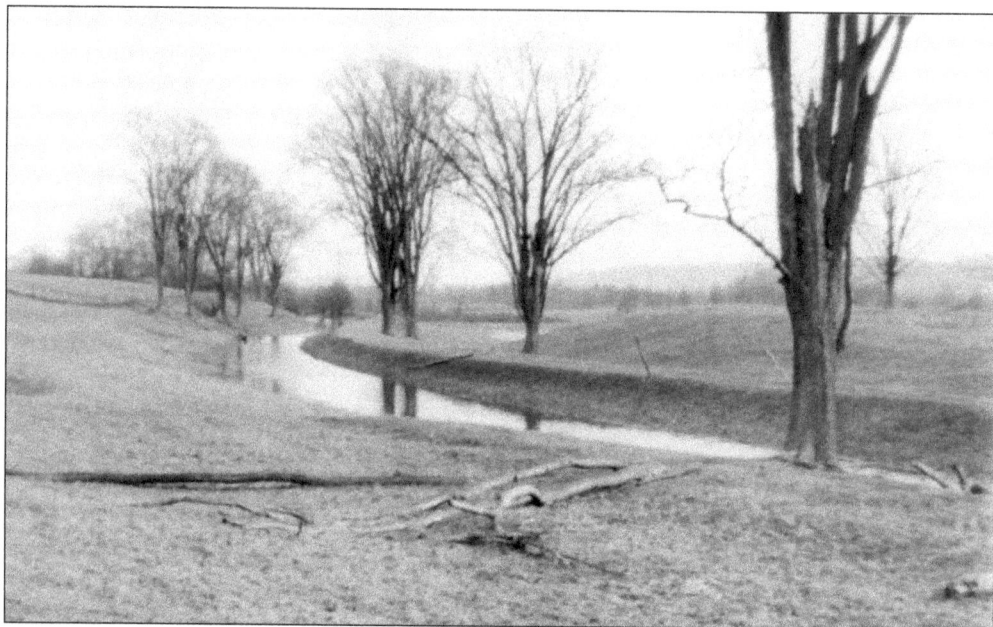

Immigrants from Ireland and Scotland were recruited to build the Chenango Canal. Their average pay was $11 per month, and they lived in temporary shanties along the banks they dug. They used inventions such as a stump-puller, which consisted of a huge set of wheels with a chain that wrapped around the stump and was leveraged around a middle wheel that turned as the oxen pulled. (Courtesy of Madison County Historical Society.)

Workers along the canal dug through quicksand, clay, and rock by hand and followed the best route chosen and designed by engineers. After $2.5 million and 41 operating years, the State of New York closed the Chenango Canal and sold off portions of it to neighboring landowners and villages. Most of it was filled in, leaving only small parts of it surviving with water. (Courtesy of Madison County Historical Society.)

Three

CIDER INDUSTRY AND MOTT'S APPLES

The Peet brothers (H.I. and E.L.) were engaged in the manufacturing of cider in Bouckville for 18 years on a small scale. They first occupied the old storehouse built by Moses Maynard when the canal was constructed. It was rebuilt and enlarged in 1876. They gave employment to some 20 persons during the duration of the two-month season and made over 10,000 barrels of cider in 1879. Three double-platform, extra-heavy Boomer & Boschert presses were used in the cider mill and were operated by a 15-horsepower engine.

Samuel Rogers Mott (born on June 29, 1826) came from Saratoga County, New York. Samuel married Ann Mary Coon and fathered five children, John Coon, Mary Frances, Frederick Gates, Samuel, and Seward. In 1866, Samuel moved his family to Burnt Hills, New York, where he became a successful fruit grower and producer of cider and vinegar. In 1868, Samuel Mott brought his family to Bouckville from Burnt Hills via the Chenango Canal during April. The Brown, Beach & Mott firm is listed in an article dated October 27, 1868, and in 1869, Samuel purchased the interest of his partners and created Mott Cider Co.

In 1879, Mott's Cider Mill, consisting of the old stone distillery and malt house on the heelpath of the Chenango Canal, was enlarged. About 9,000 barrels of cider were manufactured that year. The Peet brothers, who operated a cider mill across the canal on the towpath, agreed to sell S.R. Mott their building. New scientific methods for filtering and preserving cider were pioneered, and the oxidation process was employed for the first time. Demand for Mott's apple cider and vinegar grew. A huge complex was added along the Cherry Valley Turnpike, including a barrel-making building. A sales office was opened in New York City. Clipper ships carried 1,000-case lots of champagne cider and casks of vinegar around Cape Horn to California. By 1887, about 12–14 train carloads of apples that came from across New York State were consumed daily.

Then, in 1887, S.R. and his wife receive devastating news that an Apache Indian in Arizona had killed their youngest son, Seward, in an ambush. S.R. seemed to lose a lot of his drive for the cider business and, later, turned it over to his two older sons, John Coon Mott and Frederick Gates Mott, who called it the Genesee Fruit Company.

Samuel R. Mott occupied the old stone distillery and malt house on the heelpath of the canal. It was enlarged, principally in 1879, making its entire length about 256 feet and its width about 37 feet. A 10-horsepower engine supplied the power. This picture shows the mill along the Chenango Canal. (Courtesy of the Town of Madison Historical Society.)

In 1869, the Mott family moved to Bouckville's first built structure, McClure's Tavern, which was built by Bouckville's first merchant. S.R. Mott and his wife, Ann Mary, lived on the east side of the double house and rented the west side to two maiden ladies, Lizzie and Anna Ellison, both of whom worked for S.R. and were later bequeathed their side of the house. (Courtesy of Jim Ford.)

At the time of this photograph, taken between 1914 and 1917, the company was called the Genesee Fruit Company/Duffy's Sparkling Apple Juice. The front section of this building, located in Bouckville, New York, shows the office of the company, which faced the Cherry Valley Turnpike.

"Mott's Cider SOCONY" was referred to as the "Duffy Mott & Cider Stand." This is the cider mill looking east along the Cherry Valley Turnpike. The door at the front led into the office. Attached to the office was a small store for candy, cigarettes, sweet cider, and gas. The part of the building to the front contained the presses.

GENESEE FRUIT.Co. COOPERAGE WORKS Bouckville N

"About 300 to 350 packages, varying in size from five gallons to 30 gallons, were being turned out daily, with the entire works employing a force of 75 men or more. The cider was being shipped to points in the Eastern states and also to the West, especially Michigan," noted the *Hamilton Republican* on October 14, 1899. All products would have been coming from the "old" cooperate building shown on the left in the photograph.

This picture shows Mott's Tavern, located on the Cherry Valley Turnpike. The building was a local store for many years, and the store was later replaced with a restaurant constructed about 100 feet to the east on what has become Route 20. In this picture, one can see many bottles of cider and numerous cases of apples for sale.

Workers at the cider mill, pictured on June 2, 1929, are, from left to right, Glenn M. "Doc" Washburn, W.T. Dickinson, Patrick Brenna, and C.W. Marshall. It was quite lively around the cooperage department and also where the cider was manufactured. The new building these men are in front of was constructed in 1907 and was 150 feet long and 60 feet wide and made of cement.

These workers are inside the Mott's Cider and Vinegar plant taking a break. Mash from the distillery was fed to cows that were fattening in what were known as "still yards." The residents of Bouckville turned out in force when the fat animals were let out and started on foot for market over the turnpike.

Here is the power plant at the Genesee Fruit Company around 1900 with a load of apples. Business was lively at the Genesee Fruit Company plant, which operated 80 to 90 hours every week in the fall. About 4,000 bushels of apples were being converted into over 500 barrels of cider each day.

In 1911, the Genesee Fruit Company built its own water system by erecting a tank with a capacity of 600 barrels upon a tower 70 feet high. At the base of the tower, a cistern was constructed that also held 600 barrels of water. In this picture, one can see the "old" tower in the background, which is also shown in the prior picture from 1900.

The Duffy-Mott Company started a new industry, having put in a dry kiln for drying pomace. It shipped its first carload in 1917. This pomace is used for making jelly. The pomace, when dried, contains a large amount of pectin, which will make fruit juices jell, enabling anyone to make jelly from fruit that otherwise would not come to a jell. The company was selling it by the carload at $90 per ton.

In order to keep pace with the constant enlargement of cider/vinegar production of the Genesee Fruit Company/Duffy-Mott Company, the Ontario & Western Railroad installed the new siding to the barrel factory, a siding to the east of the facility, and a siding off the main track next to the cider mill. This new trackage gave the railroad the flexibility it needed to service the Genesee Fruit Company facility.

This picture shows the Duffy Mott Co., Inc., building, which reads, "The Largest Producers of Cider & Vinegar in Glass & Wood in the U.S.," with its bus-like display truck. This truck was taken all over the state, and perhaps beyond, to advertise and provide samples. (Courtesy of Jim Ford.)

These storage barrels were located outside the building for Genesee Fruit Company–Duffy's Sparkling Water. It is believed that in 1797, Seth Snow brought the first apple trees to Bouckville, which then became a wonderful apple-growing area. One of the first apple trees grown in the area was the "Simmons Pippin," which was brought from Rhode Island to the area by the wife of Gideon Simmons.

The cooperage plant or barrel factory was located across the tracks from the mill and well to the rear. Shown are the railroad tracks and the switch leading to the barrel factory; Crow Hill is in the background. The railroad track siding was installed by the railroad since this facility brought the railroad an increase in revenue.

These are the George Groves coal silos. The dark building to the extreme right was part of the shed for parking the horses and wagons during church services; the church is not visible in this picture. There are three sets of railroad tracks here, indicating the importance of the Mott's factory to the railroad system.

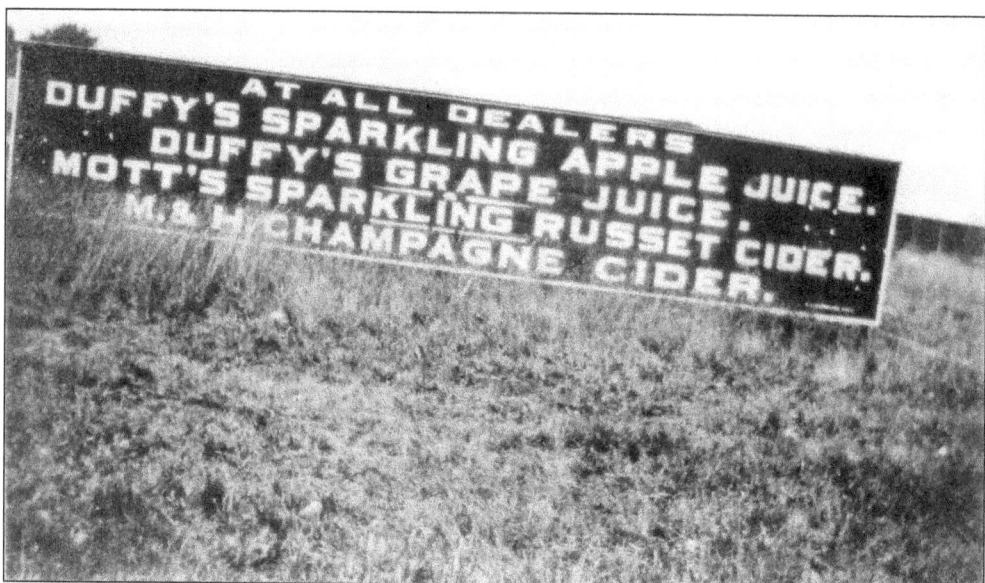

This picture shows one of the original signs located along the Cherry Valley Turnpike. When this picture was taken in 1915, the cider mill was part of the five plants in New York State: one located in Holley, one in Voorheesville, one each in Ravena and Goshen, and one in Bouckville.

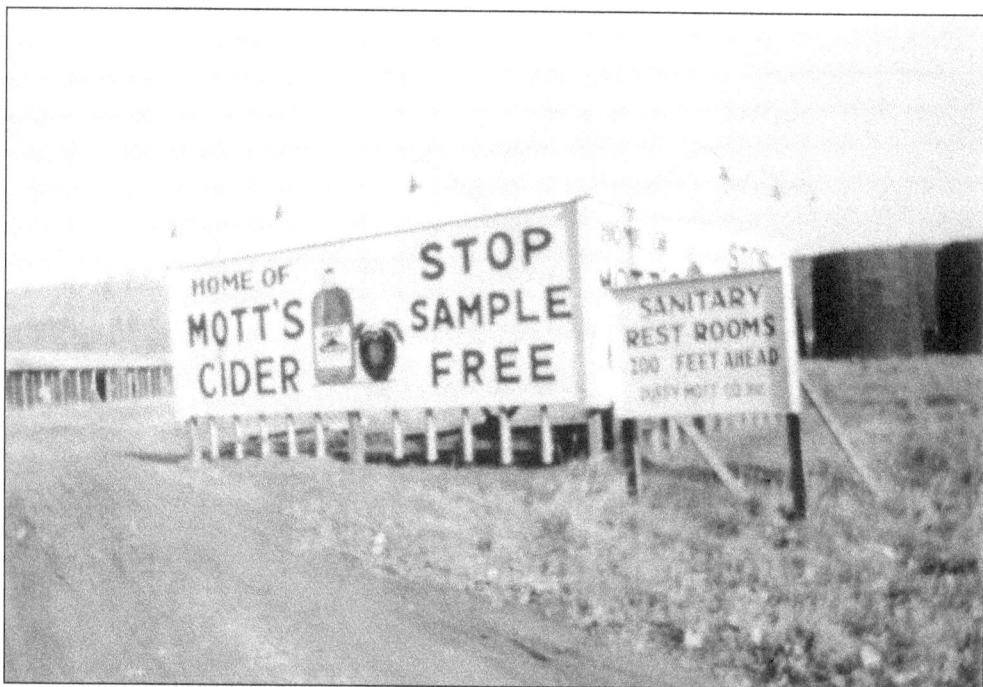

One billboard says, "Home of Mott's Cider Stop Sample Free;" the other, possibly more important, sign reads, "Sanitary Rest Rooms 200 Feet ahead Duffy Mott Co. Inc." This was in the field west of the railroad tracks on the same side of Route 20 as the cider mill. The long, low sheds to the left were used to store many things. The railroad track switch came all the way around to these sheds.

The fire at the cider mill on Route 20 on April 20, 1910, was in the rear part of the building, which was used for bottling and storing bottles of cider and vinegar. Looking carefully through the smoke just to the right of the standing firewall, one can see the church steeple. At the time, the plant was called "the Genesee Fruit Company."

The chimney to the left was part of the boiler room. The firewall (mentioned above) was two or three feet thick, there was a heavy metal sliding door on each side of the wall, and each door was well insulated. This firewall prevented the other part of the building, which contained the presses, from being destroyed in the fire.

Although local residents hoped that the plant would be rebuilt, the Duffy-Mott Company officials took a long look at the Bouckville location and decided to close the facility after the remaining inventory was sold. By now, Bouckville was far removed from the sources of apples for the mills. (Courtesy of Jim Ford.)

One of the original cider mill locations on the banks of the "old" Chenango Canal became the Bouckville Mill, Inc., also known as Summit Feeds. This 1951 aerial photograph shows the building as a mill with the canal behind it just in view to the left.

Four

RAILROADING

The New York, Ontario & Western Railroad (O&W) was laid to rest on March 29, 1957. As time marches on, it is becoming increasingly difficult to remember the railroad that has been abandoned. Employees of the road have mostly passed on, as have the folks who lived along the line and witnessed the passing trains. The O&W was in existence for 78 years. Photographs may be the best means of preserving the memory of the New York, Ontario & Western, as a camera can capture the long-gone tracks, trains, and many depots from that era.

Before railroads came to central New York, the only methods of transport were by horse-drawn wagons and canal. The railroad system was a dream just beyond the horizon. In central New York State during the first half of the 19th century, the canals were the mainstay of the manufacturing centers. The Erie Canal essentially connected Buffalo (and westward) to New York City (therefore, the East Coast) via the Hudson River. The Chenango Canal then connected Binghamton and every place in between to the West and the Atlantic Ocean. The railroad, then created on a similar route of the Chenango Canal, did the same.

A New York State law of 1850 saw the most important legislation passed to aid in the formation and construction of the railroads. It was because of this law that the New York & Oswego Midland; the Utica, Clinton & Binghamton; and many other railroads were able to form and gain financial aid for their construction. This was the birth of town bonding, a means by which municipalities could aid in the construction of the railroad and be sure it would go through their town.

Once the Civil War ended, people were able to focus on other issues and projects. New York weekly editorials promoted the need for connecting to and building railroads, which became known as "railroad fever." There were many names for the different associations that were looking to join that fever in the area, like the Oneida & Chenango Valley Railway Company; the New York & Oswego Midland Railroad; the Utica, Clinton & Binghamton Railroad (UC&B); the Delaware & Hudson Canal Company; the Lackawanna Company; and so on, which all ended up being known as the O&W, organized on January 21, 1880.

7A- NYO&WRy. STATIONS AT HAMILTON

The "new" Hamilton station was immediately a desirable subject, as seen in this 1910 scene in Hamilton. The beautifully manicured grounds surround the 11-year-old depot, while off in the distance is the original UC&B-built depot, which at this time is acting as the freight house. Whether or not one was beginning or completing a trip on the O&W here, this was the delightful setting that greeted travelers. (Courtesy of John Taibi.)

These Colgate University–trained Navy cadets will see no action, because World War II is over. The date is September 4, 1945; the Japanese surrendered two days earlier. The sailors are waiting for the approaching northbound train to pass before boarding the special train on the siding that will take them home or to peacetime duty. (Courtesy of John Taibi.)

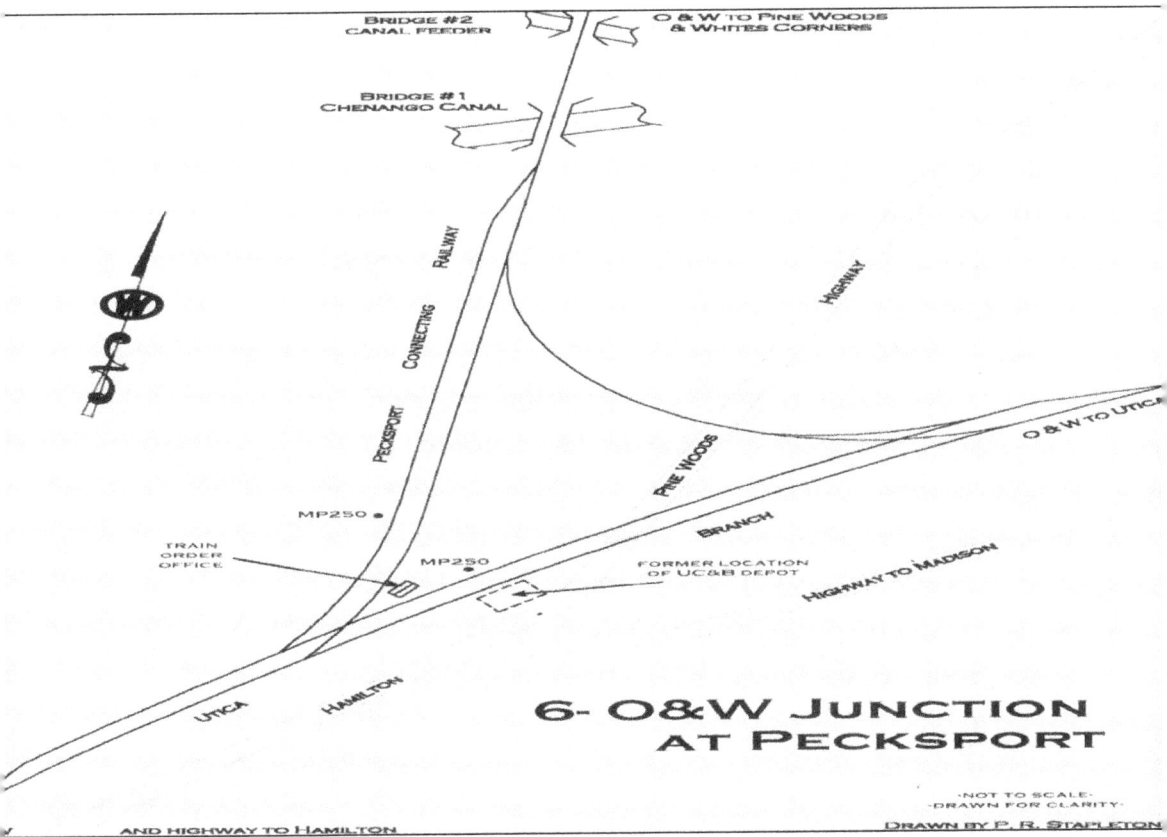

BRIDGE #2
CANAL FEEDER

O & W TO PINE WOODS
& WHITES CORNERS

BRIDGE #1
CHENANGO CANAL

PECKSPORT CONNECTING RAILWAY

HIGHWAY

O & W TO UTICA

PINE WOODS

BRANCH

MP250

TRAIN
ORDER
OFFICE

MP250

FORMER LOCATION
OF UC&B DEPOT

HIGHWAY TO MADISON

UTICA

HAMILTON

6- O&W JUNCTION
AT PECKSPORT

·NOT TO SCALE·
·DRAWN FOR CLARITY·

AND HIGHWAY TO HAMILTON

DRAWN BY P. R. STAPLETON

On August 20, 1895, general manager James E. Childs reported the following: "The construction of the loop line from Pecksport to White's Corners, entirely avoiding the long grade of seventy feet to the mile now encountered by all northbound coal and freight trains, is strongly recommended. There is no point on the Main Line where it is practical to make such a reduction of grades, and so great an average increase in the number of cars and tons hauled per train, with as little expense. An engine which now hauls 500 tons north over Eaton Summit will haul 1,030 tons over the line via Pecksport." The Pecksport Connecting Railway was organized on May 6, 1896. The grading and the laying of tracks was completed in early August, and the line was ready for use on September 13, 1896. (Courtesy of John Taibi.)

In preparing for the Pecksport Loop to be opened to traffic on September 13, 1896, train order offices were built at both ends of the 3.69-mile line. The office at Pecksport was situated within the junction that the loop joining the Utica Division main line formed. (Courtesy of John Taibi.)

On a late-spring afternoon in 1913, O&W employees pose for their photograph on the Pecksport Connecting Railway side of the train order office in Pecksport. Even though only C. Leon Clifford (left) is identified, the picture is still very interesting. (Courtesy of John Taibi.)

The original Bouckville depot was one of three station houses built by the Utica, Clinton & Binghamton Railroad whose specifications were nearly identical. Bouckville's end entranceway was on the north side of the building facing the Cherry Valley Turnpike. This gave access to the waiting room. The original Bouckville depot, along with the adjoining coal sheds, was destroyed by fire on September 15, 1911. (Courtesy of John Taibi.)

After fire destroyed the UC&B depot at Bouckville, Lyon Mills built this handsome new station for the O&W at a cost of $5,975. It was opened to the public as of January 1913. The church with its steeple on the right of this photograph still remains, but the George Groves coal silos on the left in this photograph are just a memory. (Courtesy of John Taibi.)

By the time of the Ontario & Western's last full year of operation in 1956, the "newer" O&W-built depots were already 44 to 57 years old; fortunately, many were saved, such as this one in Bouckville. The depot became Quacks Diner, "one of the best places to stop on US Route 20 in Bouckville," as indicated in its advertising. The tracks were torn up, yet the building remains to this day. (Courtesy of Jim Ford.)

The No. 20 train is leaving Bouckville and heading south toward Pecksport and the loop. Since railroads prefer to operate their trains over as level a grade as they can, it was only natural that the O&W would try to lop off part of the Midland's Eaton Hill Summit. The Pecksport Loop did this.

The Borden Milk plant was located on the tracks in Bouckville with several spurs so that the trains could stop to pick up the farmers' milk. According to Helen "Aunt Hetty" Washburn's diary, on January 4, 1904, it was "30 degrees below zero, Midnight train did not come till morning & milk train had two engines."

This is the milk station looking from the north to the south toward Hamilton along the O&W Railroad tracks. The milk station was actually on the offshoot of the main tracks. This offshoot went to the depot but dead-ended. The train had to back up south on the track and pick up the main rail. This picture was taken in 1915.

During this early period of depot development, state of the art meant a box-shaped structure built entirely of wood, whose outside sheathing of boards and battens was used to cover a skeletal wood-beamed frame. Solsville was one of three built like this (the others being Bouckville & Oriskany Falls). There was no entranceway directly into the agent's office from the outside. (Courtesy of John Taibi.)

When the Utica, Clinton & Binghamton Railroad opened, it had employed state-of-the-art architectural designs in constructing its rural station houses. In this picture is the state-of-the-art Solsville depot, which was last under the care of Ontario & Western agent Lavina "Lulubelle" Starkweather. (Courtesy of John Taibi.)

On the rainy evening of September 25, 1955, a nasty wreck happened on the O&W in Hamilton. The circumstances surrounding this wreck, which did not claim any lives, include surprise, fear, mystery, astonishment, mistaken accusation, a high school student, and a lighter-than-air diesel locomotive. (Courtesy of John Taibi.)

Over the years, this wreck has been referred to as "the Chocolate Wreck" and the "Wreck of the Flying Diesel Corps." This one accident has remained in the forefront of O&W history. It is an unbelievable story of how an unidentified person threw the switch for the Leland Coal Company siding and sent southbound train ON-2 up the siding and into the coal shed. (Courtesy of John Taibi.)

This was fondly known as "the Chocolate Wreck" because several of the freight cars that came crashing to the ground contained Nestlé Crunch bars from that company's plant in Fulton, New York. The chocolate bars littered the scene, and before officials could secure the area, the village kids (and adults alike) made off with their delicious booty. (Courtesy of John Taibi.)

This was the worst wreck on the Utica Division. The only thing that kept it from being a tragedy was that none of the four crewmen riding in the cab perished. The cause of the wreck is wrapped in mystery, and since candy stores in Hamilton almost went out of business afterwards, it is still one of the most talked about and well-remembered wrecks. (Courtesy of John Taibi.)

Five

PEOPLE OF INTEREST

Many farmers, hops being a primary crop thanks to James Coolidge, occupied Madison and Hamilton. One such farmer, Noah Washburn I, moved from Bridgewater, Massachusetts, to Bouckville, in the town of Madison, around 1796, and brought with him his wife, Eunice Blodgett, and four children. They had five more children in Bouckville. Noah purchased two large parcels of land, one in 1814 and the other in 1815.

Noah Washburn II was born in 1796 and was the son of Noah Washburn I, who was born in 1764. The Washburn lineage can be traced back to the year 495 and includes interesting ancestors such as the Duke of Brittany; King Louis IV of France, born in 921; and Cerdic, who landed in Britain in 495 and in six years subdued the natives in what became the Kingdom of the West Saxons or Wessex.

Noah Washburn I passed parcels of land in Bouckville to his three sons, Noah II, Zaddock, and Marcius in 1846. On April 29, 1856, Zaddock and Marcius signed over the interest of their parcels on Crow Hill Road to their brother, Noah II. Farming was their way of life, with the main crop being hops. Marcius Cady Washburn, who married Sophia Ann Parker, retained a parcel in Bouckville proper. Their daughter Helen Sophia ("Aunt Hetty") did extensive genealogy research and was a spinster who shared the research with her nephews.

On December 18, 1886 (two years before he died), Noah II deeded his land over to his wife (Adaline J. Hitchcock) and five children. He actually had six children; the youngest, Henry, died at age 5. The other five children were Leavitt, Mary Delisle, Woodford Paul, Martha Eunice and Alice Adeline. By this time, they may have been just as dependant on milk from the farm as the hops.

In 1890, Woodford and his wife, Cordelia, along with Martha and her husband, Scoville Marshall, deeded their interest in the land over to Dan W. Forward (son of Mary Delisle), Leavitt Washburn, and Alice Washburn.

This picture is of Noah Washburn II and Adeline J. Hitchcock Washburn around 1879. Their children, Alice, Leavitt, and Delisle, deeded their interest in the land on Crow Hill Road over to Dan Washburn Forward, who became the sole owner.

William Henry Washburn, pictured here, was born about 1822 in Madison County. He was the son of Leavitt Washburn (the eldest son of Noah Washburn Sr.) and Betsey Love. Leavitt died at a young age, leaving Betsey with four daughters and one son, William Henry. After living for a period in Madison County, Betsey and her children moved to Forestville in Chautauqua County about 1837.

This is the family of Marvin Emory and Elise Marie Phelps Washburn. The picture was taken in 1900 at Summit Stock Farm in Bouckville. From left to right, Florence Elsie was born in 1882; Marvin Emory Washburn was born in 1853; Robert Phelps was born in 1896; Elsie Marie Phelps Washburn was born in 1869. Elsie is holding Melville Charles, who was born 1899; Leslie Marcius was born in 1888; Glen "Doc" Marvin was born in 1881. The Washburns were a big part of the cider industry as well as the baseball team.

The Summits baseball team from Bouckville were the amateur champions of Central New York in 1907. In this picture are, from left to right, (standing) Arthur J. Wiltse, Leo Wiltse, Leslie Washburn, Will Edgarton, and "Skid" Livermore; (sitting) Glenn Stringer, Will Hillicker, "Squire" Howard, Glenn "Doc" Washburn, and Sam Collister. (Courtesy of Jim Ford.)

Here is another picture of the Summits baseball team taken between 1912 and 1914. Pictured are, from left to right, (first row) Will Edgarton, Lyle Stringer, Emery Howard (the manager), Bob Washburn (the batboy), Glenn Washburn, and Liba Martin; (second row) James Livermore, Earl Parker, Harry Washburn, Albert Edgarton, and Seward Guillaume. (Courtesy of Jim Ford.)

Standing outside of the Bouckville Mill, Inc., on Canal Road, Bouckville, in 1959, are, from left to right, Ed Baker, Bob Bennett, Wally Zoffert, Dan Lynch, and Lyle Jeffries. Feed from this mill was delivered to the local farmers in bulk, as advertised on the side of the truck. Not visible in this copy of the photograph is Jack Cary.

Capt. J.H. Waterman communicated with Canadian government officials, who gave him permission to obtain two buffalo calves at $50 each. The captain and his two sons went to northern Canada in order to bring the buffaloes to Madison. They were about eight months old and weighed about 350 pounds each. After extreme difficulty, Waterman trained the buffaloes with the help of Harold Forward of Bouckville. (Courtesy of the Town of Madison Historical Society.)

The buffaloes were named Ned and Ted by Capt. J.H. Waterman. For several summers, Waterman gave regular afternoon shows at his farm. In 1942, he exhibited his remarkable team at the Brookfield Fair for the first time. Though this photograph says Deansboro, New York, he had the buffaloes staked by Route 20 at the intersection with Center Road in Madison four summers in a row. (Courtesy of the Town of Madison Historical Society.)

In 1943, Waterman and his buffaloes appeared with the James M. Cole Circus for 24 weeks, traveling through six states. He put them through their paces at the Great Barrington, Massachusetts, fair in 1944 and exhibited them at the Brookfield Fair again that autumn. (Courtesy of the Town of Madison Historical Society.)

Grove W. Hinman was born on September 11, 1889, and died on March 14, 1961. On May 4, 1944, the *Hamilton Republican* reported the following: "Hats off to Morris Sherman and Grove Hinman! They have combined their efforts to provide more comfortable housing and health conditions for the Negroes who will help harvest crops this season. The infirmary building on the Hinman farm north of Hamilton, on the Bouckville road, will be converted (from a chicken coop) into a school for young children. It will be supervised by a competent teacher." On March 14, 1961, it reported that Grove W. Hinman, reputed to be Madison County's wealthiest farmer and businessman, died at age 71 at his home in Madison. (Courtesy of Jim Ford.)

The *Hamilton Republican* of April 4, 1935, reported: "Mr. G.W. Hinman has commenced work on the new garage to be built on the property recently purchased of Mrs. A.L. Jones. The house is to be removed to a lot purchased of Mrs. Ella Head" located on Route 20 in the village of Madison. The garage sold Gulf gas. (Courtesy of the Town of Madison Historical Society.)

G.W. Hinman moved his office from Solsville to the new garage on East Main Street in Madison in January 1936. New fixtures and office furniture made the place very attractive. Agnes Pilbeam was in charge of the office. Hinman continued the same line of business, namely coal, gas, oil, and trucking, and ran a regular service and repair station. (Courtesy of the Town of Madison Historical Society.)

Madison Central School (MCS) bus drivers during the school year of 1951–1952 included, from left to right, Glenn Quackenbush, of Quacks Diner; Jack Johnson, owner of a Dodge dealership; Dave Kennett, son of the man who started Kennett's Garage in Knoxboro; Don Carney, the husband of the district clerk for MCS; Fordie Phillips, the justice of the peace; and Lee Williams, of Lee's Texaco. (Courtesy of the Town of Madison Historical Society.)

Pictured here is Lee P. Williams, who, with his wife Katherine (Forward) Williams, opened Lee's Texaco in Madison next to Quacks Diner. He later moved it west on Route 20 near Route 12B between Madison and Bouckville. Lee worked for Jack Johnson at his Dodge dealership for a while after getting out of the service. (Courtesy of Kay Williams.)

Gen. Erastus Cleaveland arrived in the township area in 1793. He purchased a farm and settled a mile below the area that became Solsville. After he built a series of mills, the area became known as Cleaveland Mills. He is pictured here with his wife, Rebecca. (Courtesy of Madison County Historical Society.)

James D. Coolidge married six times—Janet Kendall in 1814, Sophia Stebbins in 1819, Sallie Simmons in 1833, Harriett Hazzard in 1834, Phoebe Tompkins Lawrence in 1842, and Mary Coburn Smith in 1851—and all of his wives died prior to James. It was because of Coolidge's success with hops that others soon followed, and by the 1820s, the hop industry was firmly implanted into the agricultural landscape of the area. (Courtesy of Madison County Historical Society.)

This group of roughly 40 students with two or three teachers makes up the entire population of the Bouckville School in 1890. Bouckville was the second school to organize in the district. It was known as District No. 10. The Bouckville School was originally a cobblestone building on the corner of the Cherry Valley Turnpike and Maple Street. (Courtesy of Jim Ford.)

These are the pupils of the Bouckville School in 1935. Pictured with teacher Lillian Coe are, from left to right, (first row) Dan Forward, Donald Morey, Hazel LaFleur, Lois Dahn, Carter Young, Jimmie Lillie, Bob Washburn, and Peggy Cleary; (second row) John Mesinna, Katherine Forward, Evelyn Mae Babcock, Janice Fuess, and Frances Cleary. (Courtesy of the Town of Madison Historical Society.)

No longer in the school, these Bouckville men are pictured in 1905. The history of the school system in the area began on June 19, 1812, when the government of the State of New York passed legislation that each township of the state was to be divided into common school districts. (Courtesy of Jim Ford.)

These young women of Bouckville are also out of school in 1905. The schools were generally one-room schools, and one teacher instructed the students. Usually, students attended from the first grade through the eighth grade and then entered the work force. Once in the work force, they looked for recreation in their Sunday best, as shown here. (Courtesy of Jim Ford.)

Six

Bouckville Hamlet

Bouckville is situated near the center of the west border of the town of Madison, located at one time on the line of the Utica, Clinton & Binghamton Railroad and the Chenango Canal, which passes through a deep cutting at this place. As of 1880, Bouckville contained one church (Methodist Episcopal), a district school (built about 1876, at a cost of some $1,600), one hotel (known as the White House and kept by William Edgarton), one store, a steam sawmill and cheese box factory, two extensive cider mills, two blacksmith shops (Chauncey Clark and Columbus Lewis), a shoe shop (D.W. Smith), and 50 dwellings. It is six miles from Hamilton and two miles from Madison.

Bouckville has enjoyed the distinction of various names. It was first known as McClure Settlement, from the McClure Tavern located there, and, contemporaneously, as the Hook. Later, at a drunken carousal, it was christened Johnsville in honor of John Edgarton, the first settler on its site. When the post office was established, it received its present name in honor of William C. Bouck, the then–canal commissioner.

The first merchant at Bouckville was Dr. Samuel McClure, who came from Vermont with his family of eight children about 1805. He purchased a farm on the site of the village, covering the greater part of lot No. 2, on which the village is principally located. He built a small frame store that stood in the garden attached to the residence of James Coolidge but traded only a year or two. He then moved to Erie County and invented a nail machine. He did not engage in trade until during the War of 1812, beginning about 1813. His son David remained a year or two and then moved to the Mississippi Country.

Ira Burhans was the next merchant of importance. He came from the Hudson country about 1854 and traded in company with his son Lindorf until the opening of the Civil War, about 1861. The elder Burhams returned to Albany County. William Coolidge succeeded Lindorf Burhans and continued till his death on June 5, 1875. He was the youngest son of James D. Coolidge, an early settler, and brother of the venerable James Coolidge.

This picture was taken in Bouckville looking east along the Cherry Valley Turnpike to Madison. The train was still running at this time, as the railroad crossing is still visible in the distance. The telephone poles indicate there is electricity through the hamlet.

This is a nice bird's-eye view of the hamlet of Bouckville. It shows several significant buildings, such as the Landmark and the White House on either side of the Cherry Valley Turnpike. Lewis E. Coe, a native of Madison, opened a store in the hamlet in February 1876. (Courtesy of the Town of Madison Historical Society.)

This picture was taken from the Chenango Canal Bridge looking up "Main Street," as is written on the photograph, in Bouckville, New York. Main Street in this picture is actually the Cherry Valley Turnpike, present-day Route 20. The White House is on the left; Coe & Brockett Store (the Landmark) is on the right.

This is a nice view of the White House, as it was called at the time the picture was taken on June 29, 1900. It was captured from across the Cherry Valley Turnpike. The White House (later called the Bouckville Hotel) still had the large addition seen on the right. This addition was later removed.

69

This is a wonderful close-up picture of the Coe & Brockett Store in Bouckville. It was next called "the Old Stone Store," then became the Landmark and Ye Old Landmark Tavern. This photograph shows the entrances to each of the sections. At the time of the photograph, it was divided into four sections, one of which was the post office.

This is one of the homes on the Parker brothers' farm. This house belonged to Mrs. Frank Parker. As the postcard says, Parker's Lodging offered meals to lodgers on the Cherry Valley Turnpike, located in "Bouchville, NY." (Bouckville being misspelled on the postcard). (Courtesy of the Town of Madison Historical Society.)

This postcard tells that this is "the Parker Farm, Mrs. Frank Parker. Rooms for tourists—meals—bath—free garage—heat. On the Cherry Valley Turnpike, Route 20—Phone Madison 8-F-4, Bouckville, NY." In this photograph, one can see the second Parker brothers' farmhouse. The houses were built to look identical from the outside. (Courtesy of the Town of Madison Historical Society.)

Here is a front view of Mrs. Frank Parker's home on the Parker brother's farm in Bouckville, New York, located on what became State Route 20. As shown on this postcard, the Parker Farm provided "Rooms—Meals—Bath." These three pictures of the Parker home were actually taken at different times, as indicated by the different signs out front. (Courtesy of the Town of Madison Historical Society.)

This picture shows A.P. White (left) and Earl Parker, the owners of Ryan Leland and Company, which became the Bouckville Mill. The picture was taken on March 22, 1938, a very hot 74-degree day and the same year the author's father was born into this quaint hamlet on April 1. (Courtesy of the Town of Madison Historical Society.)

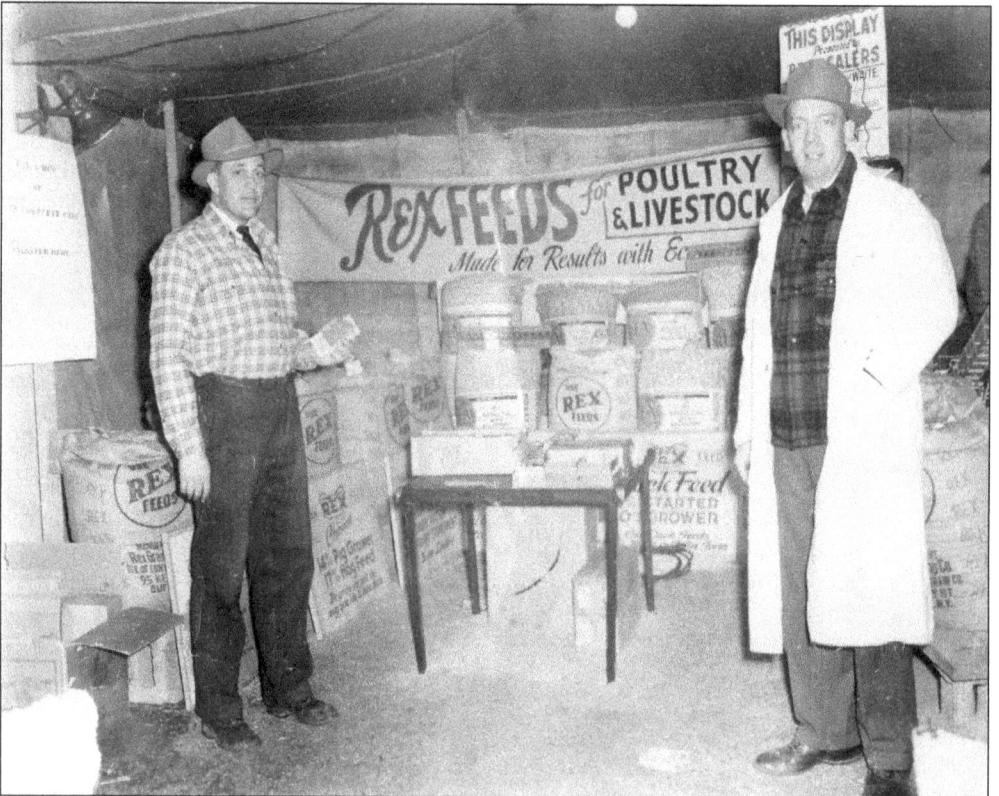

Inside the Bouckville Mill advertising Rex feeds are owners Bob Bennett (left) and Ed Baker. The phone number was Madison Twin Oaks 3-3211. This building was erected by Duffy Mott Company to process apple cider and became a feed mill about 1915. The picture says, "In stock, Stanford Seeds; Matheison Ammo Phos Fertilizers; American Red Point Barbed wire; Fence Posts & Fence supplies. Take them direct to the field, no extra handling, same early prices." (Courtesy of the Town of Madison Historical Society.)

Colgate University's 30-man unit of the Civil Aeronautics Authority began activity on October 10, 1940, with 23 seniors, five juniors, and two men not enrolled in college. Three Piper Cub planes, furnished by Niagara From the Air, Inc., were used in the 1,050 hours of flight training given during the first semester. The airplane hangar was used by Colgate University for pilot training during World War II. (Courtesy of the Town of Madison Historical Society.)

The Airport Inn was located on Route 20 at the Junction of 12B (near the Colgate University airport hangar). The inn served luncheons and dinners as well as bridge and dinner parties. The cocktail lounge was owned by Mildred and Earl Cossaboom, and the phone number was Madison 79. The Airport Inn was later known as Cossaboom's Restaurant. (Courtesy of the Town of Madison Historical Society.)

On February 17, 1938, Bouckville native Burt H. Pierce's invention, designed to eliminate use of radiators on automobiles with a substitute form of artificial refrigeration, was in the hands of the American Bureau of Invention in New York City. This picture, taken in 1950s, is of Pierce's garage. (Courtesy of the Town of Madison Historical Society.)

Another garage in the Bouckville area was Otto Fisher's Garage, as depicted in this picture taken in 1920 from Indian Opening Road. Otto had the first automobile "pit" in the area. The customer would drive the car into the garage, straddling the pit, and Otto would go down the steps under the automobile to check it out from underneath. (Courtesy of the Town of Madison Historical Society.)

Looking from the south to the north toward Bouckville on the "road" side is the milk station. The farmers brought their milk under the overhang on the west side of the station to sell. This picture was taken some time between 1910 and 1917. Fay Forward delivered milk to this station into the 1950s, when she then went back to taking milk to Solsville. This was then an ice cream plant for a while.

The school bell of the Bouckville White School, which had rung without interruption for 70 years, was silenced forever when it was voted to send teacher and pupils to the Madison Central School. For the last time, it pealed out loud and clear on February 22, 1939, when Lillian Coe supervised a brief program within the little building. (Courtesy of the Town of Madison Historical Society.)

The Methodist Episcopal Church of Bouckville was organized in 1853; its house of worship was erected at a cost of $2,500 that same year. The original members were Solomon Root, Mr. and Mrs. Solomon Root Jr., Mr. and Mrs. D. Root, G. Root, Mr. and Mrs. A.G. Fargo, George Patterson, H. Patterson, Mrs. William W. Woodhull, Mrs. James Edgarton, Mrs. F.J. Tooke, and Mr. and Mrs. E. Newcomb. (Courtesy of the Town of Madison Historical Society.)

This picture is of the Methodist Episcopal Church of Bouckville after the two doors were removed and made into one middle door, as shown here. During the first two years, circuit preachers ministered to the congregation—the first year, Reverends Clark and Graves, and the second year, Reverends Beebe and Higgins. (Courtesy of the Town of Madison Historical Society.)

Though the picture says "Canal St.," it is labeled incorrectly. This photograph is of Crow Hill Road, where the road meets up with the Cherry Valley Turnpike. The sidewalk along the right-hand side divided the road from the Chenango Canal, though the canal was down an embankment. (Courtesy of the Town of Madison Historical Society.)

This photograph is of Maple Avenue in the area where the "Little White" Bouckville School was located, though it is not shown. It would have been on the right side and at about the spot of the photographer. One could get to the milk station by going down this road. (Courtesy of the Town of Madison Historical Society.)

"Brockers Store and Post Office on Main Street, Bouckville, NY," is what is written on the back of this photograph. The main road going through Bouckville was known as the Cherry Valley Turnpike. The store is the first building pictured on the left. Farther down the road in the picture is part of the Mott's complex.

This is Frank Parker's Saloon, with Frank leaning on the stairs. The photograph was taken in September 1911; the saloon was located on the Cherry Valley Turnpike going through the hamlet of Bouckville, New York. Saloons were great places to go and visit with other townsfolk. This is the same Parker family that has been mentioned in other photographs.

This building was known as the Stone Store and was located on the corner of Route 20 and Route 46 in what is called Pine Woods. The stones used to build this store-and-house combination were brought up the canal to Bouckville and then moved by horse and wagon to this site, a total distance of 1.5 miles. (Courtesy of the Town of Madison Historical Society.)

This picture states, "Wilkinson's Inn Service Station, Modern Heated Cabins—Showers—Lunches—Gas—Oil Route 20 Pine Woods, Bouckville, NY." On the top of the building, the signs read, "Pine Woods Inn Modern Cabins" and "Texaco" gas. This is located next to the Pine Woods Church, which is visible on the right in this photograph. (Courtesy of Helen Nower.)

Seven

SOLSVILLE HAMLET

Solsville is situated in the northwest part of the town of Madison, about three-quarters of a mile north of the village of Madison and two miles below Bouckville. It lies in the deep gully of Oriskany Creek, which furnished limited waterpower, and was on the railroad line and the canal. It contained a gristmill, a hotel, a blacksmith shop, a wagon shop, a tin shop, a grocery, and two shoe shops at its peak.

Solsville derived its name from early settler Solomon Alcott. It was once a thriving, enterprising place, but the abandonment of the canal and the opening of the railroad materially affected its interests. A wealthy farming population surrounds it.

The first merchant in Solsville was Nathaniel S. Howard, who traded there in a small way during the time he held the mill property with his brother Ambrose from about 1831 to 1839. The next was Abel Curtis and his uncle Thompson Curtis, who traded from 1832 to 1835. In 1835, Abel Curtis and Marsden Kershaw formed a partnership under the name of Curtis & Kershaw, which continued until 1838, when Kershaw purchased Curtis's interest. After about a year, Kershaw associated himself with Amasa Paddleford and operated under the name of Kershaw & Co., which lasted about a year and ended with Kershaw purchasing Paddleford's interest to form a partnership with Kershaw's brother Robert.

They continued under the same name until 1861, when Robert withdrew, and Marsden Kershaw sold a half interest to Benjamin S. Bridge. The name became and remained Kershaw & Bridge until 1869, when Bridge sold his interest to Augustus N. Peckham. Within a year, Kershaw sold his interest to John Harris and the store to Julius Tucker. Harris & Peckham traded about 10 months when Harris bought out Peckham, continuing about two years.

Warren H. Benjamin & Son commenced trading in the spring of 1875. When Harris went out, dry goods ceased to be a branch of the business.

The first postmaster at Solsville was Albert Hall, who was succeeded by Marsden Kershaw, who held the office eight years. Agur Gilbert was the next postmaster for six months until 1864, when Isaac Phelps was appointed.

In the forefront of this photograph is the farm of Benjamin Phelps, located on a hill that leads into the village of Madison to the south and to Solsville to the north. Additionally, looking northeast, one can see the prosperous farmland of the Solsville area with white fencing for keeping the animals contained. (Courtesy of the Town of Madison Historical Society.)

This is an aerial view of Solsville with the mills, train, and depot along with Mill Pond. This photograph shows the original bridge going over the Chenango Canal. The bridge was a Burr truss; the design was patented in 1817. (Courtesy of the Town of Madison Historical Society.)

Here are the original train station in the background and original mill buildings in the foreground—all long gone. The picturesque structures of the canal bridges (seen to the left) were generally of the same design, varying only in size. Each bridge sat on stone abutments, and the wooden roadway that stretched across was supported by a wooden truss. (Courtesy of the Town of Madison Historical Society.)

Here is Mill Pond showing the bridge going over the Chenango Canal as it was when in operation. Additionally, one can see the Burr truss bridge, which consisted of a truss with parallel top and bottom chords and, in between, single or double diagonals and two timber arch ribs, one on each side of the roadway. (Courtesy of the Town of Madison Historical Society.)

5—Main Street, Solsville, N. Y.

As the photograph says, this is "Main Street" in Solsville. The Solsville Hotel is on the left and a store is on right, which also contained the post office. What is being labeled as Main Street in this photograph is actually called Valley Road and runs the valley along the canal to Bouckville. (Courtesy of the Town of Madison Historical Society.)

This photograph is of the inside of the Solsville Store and Post Office, taken in 1931. The postmaster shown in this photograph is George Lathrop, who was appointed on March 22, 1929. This building is located across from where the Van Veckler home was located before it was torn down in 1974. The cellar of the Van Veckler home was used to store boats for the Chenango Canal days. (Courtesy of the Town of Madison Historical Society.)

This photograph shows the "old" mill. The Solsville gristmill was built around 1810 by Gen. Erastus Cleaveland, who was succeeded in ownership by his son-in-law Nathan Niles Howard. During the latter's occupancy, it stood idle some 18 years pending Howard's efforts to obtain remuneration from the state for damages sustained by the opening of the canal. (Courtesy of the Town of Madison Historical Society.)

Here are the bridge and milldam. Canal boats surely did not go over that! Howard received some $10,000 from the state from three different appraisements. On Howard's death on January 21, 1855, the property passed to his brother Adin. (Courtesy of the Town of Madison Historical Society.)

Looking toward Bouckville is a view of the dam holding back the millpond. Soon after he acquired it, Adin Howard transferred ownership of the mill to A.C. Wheeler, who refitted it, put in new machinery, and operated it for a few years. (Courtesy of the Town of Madison Historical Society.)

This picture, looking toward Madison on the right, shows the back of the old mill and Mill Pond. A.C. Wheeler sold the mill to William A. Simmons, who, after two or three years, sold to William S. Pierce, who sold it to James H. Parker. (Courtesy of the Town of Madison Historical Society.)

This photograph shows the old mill after the dam of the Chenango Canal burst on June 11, 1917. A dozen houses, barns, and warehouses, besides scores of smaller structures, were either crushed or carried downstream. Thousands of feet of lumber, in fact the entire stock of Dolan's yard, were swept away. (Courtesy of Ron and Viola Neff.)

The bursting of the dam caused extensive damage to everything around it in the Solsville area. The catastrophe occurred shortly after 6:00 a.m. due to three milldams at and just below Solsville giving way. All three dams held back waters, creating large ponds. There was a great confusion among the villages in the path of the oncoming flood. (Courtesy of Ron and Viola Neff.)

This photograph, looking west, shows the Solsville Hotel with hop bines growing on it. Solsville is known for its historic Solsville Hotel, which was at one point the town post office, saloon, and ballroom and is currently home to a restaurant and a popular Irish pub owned by B. Dixon. (Courtesy of the Town of Madison Historical Society.)

This photograph was taken coming from Bouckville via Valley Road along the canal and looking down "Main Street" into the hamlet of Solsville. Note the store in the distance on the right. The old canal house was located behind the store in Solsville, which has been converted into a bar. (Courtesy of the Town of Madison Historical Society.)

This is the Borden Milk Plant that was located in Solsville, New York. Gail Borden Jr., the company's founder, was born in 1801 in Norwich, New York. Despite the apparent usefulness of condensed milk, the US Patent Office rejected Borden's patent application three times. It was finally accepted on August 19, 1856. (Courtesy of the Town of Madison Historical Society.)

This photograph shows Borden Milk Plant workers at Solsville. They are, from left to right, Art Anderson, Wesley Pilbeam, and Floyd Welch. Gail Borden Jr. died in 1874, leaving management of the thriving company to his sons John Gail and Henry Lee. William J. Rogers took over in 1902. S. Frederick Taylor, who was concentrating on the company's stronghold in New York, succeeded him in 1910. (Courtesy of the Town of Madison Historical Society.)

This photograph shows one of the two Solsville schools. The schools of the town of Madison, which became part of the Madison Central System, included this building, which was labeled as District No. 11. This school was a quarter-mile north of Solsville on the Solsville-Augusta Road. (Courtesy of the Town of Madison Historical Society.)

This is a close up of what is considered the Old Feed Mill in Solsville, originally owned by Nathaniel Howard. Mills and factories sprang up along the southern end of the Chenango Canal, while stores and hotels were established all along the retail corridor. Numerous and varied supporting businesses also flourished, including taverns, inns, and boatyards. (Courtesy of the Town of Madison Historical Society.)

90

Eight

VILLAGE OF MADISON

The village of Madison lies in the town of Madison, which is bordered on the north by Stockbridge and Augusta, east by Sangerfield and Brookfield, south by Hamilton, and west by Eaton, and totals 22,500 acres.

In 1792, Solomon Perkins purchased 500 acres near what is Madison Lake, where the Indians had camped, fished, and hunted for centuries. Here, at Indian Opening, the first white settlement had its start in 1792.

At the same time, a second community was formed at Madison Center. James Collester opened the Bulls Head Tavern in 1793, and by 1810, many small businesses and industries had been established in the center.

Seth Gibson first took up the land upon which the village of Madison is located; however, John Berry is considered the founder of Madison in 1801.

Erastus Cleaveland, one of Madison's original pioneers, established mills along the Oriskany Creek in 1792. He was Madison's first supervisor for two terms and was elected president of the board. He was the brigadier general for the county's militia. He served at Sackett's Harbor and the War of 1812. He started a distillery and brewery and, later, a carding machine and satinet cloth factory. He also dealt in buying and fattening cattle for New York and Philadelphia markets.

James D. Coolidge of Stow, Middlesex County, Massachusetts, came to Madison in 1806. He purchased a farm from John Niles on lot No. 43. The Madison-Bouckville Antique Show is located on lot No. 43 today. This farm is the first farm off Route 20 on Route 12B headed south. The farm he bought was one of the best in the town of Madison; it once took the County Agricultural Society's premium of a silver cup.

One of the town's natural assets is Madison Lake, the location for the area's summer resorts and for hops picnics.

Grove W. Hinman was one of Central New York's largest farm operators in the 1940s and 1950s, specializing in diary and vegetables.

Today, Madison is known for its wealth of antique and auction concerns. The area between Madison and Bouckville on Route 20 is popularly referred to as the "Madison-Bouckville Antique Community" and hosts many shops.

This is the village of Madison's business section in 1920. Looking west along the Cherry Valley Turnpike are Spooner's Grocery Store, which was later owned by the Gazzals, and the Collister House. A tragic fire took out a good section of this block in 1986. (Courtesy of the Town of Madison Historical Society.)

This is the same 1920 business section of Madison but looking east along the Cherry Valley Turnpike. It is interesting to see paved sidewalks yet dirt roads. Note that one building has firewalls. (Courtesy of the Town of Madison Historical Society.)

This is the inside of Robert Clark's blacksmith shop in 1910. Clark created products out of wrought iron, and despite common usage, the person who shoes horses is called a farrier, rather than a blacksmith. Many farriers carried out both trades, as did Robert Clark. (Courtesy of the Town of Madison Historical Society.)

This picture, taken in 1910, is the Octagon Cobblestone House, located in the village of Madison and owned by Louis Fuess at the time. This is "the other" octagon house often referred to in articles written about James Coolidge and his house, which did not turn out to be a true octagon. (Courtesy of the Town of Madison Historical Society.)

This photograph was taken while standing on the Cherry Valley Turnpike looking down South Street in the village of Madison in 1911. A traveler could take this road to get to Madison Center in one direction or continue to Lake Moraine and beyond to the village and town of Hamilton. (Courtesy of the Town of Madison Historical Society.)

This photograph reads "East Street, Madison, NY." Though the photographer is looking east, this would be the Cherry Valley Turnpike. The photograph was taken from the corner of South Street, near Spooner's Grocery Store, in 1911. (Courtesy of the Town of Madison Historical Society.)

94

The signs over this garage in 1932 read as follows: "Reynolds Garage–Plymouth" and "Sales Dodge Service." The building was known as Dunster Hall and as Fuess Hall before Herm Reynolds bought it. School was held here in former years as well as community meetings and band rehearsals. (Courtesy of the Town of Madison Historical Society.)

Pictured looking west from the four corners of Madison is the digging of the Cherry Valley Turnpike. These Italian workers helped pave the first cement road in Madison County, constructed from the bridge in Bouckville to the village of Oriskany Falls, in 1914; the road was widened in 1931. (Courtesy of the Town of Madison Historical Society.)

This is the Madison Baptist Church, erected in 1833 and located on North Street in the village of Madison. The first town meeting for Madison was held on March 3, 1807, and Levi Morton was the supervisor between 1829 and 1840, when this church was erected. (Courtesy of the Town of Madison Historical Society.)

This is the Madison Congregational Church, which was erected 1820 and located on South Street in Madison. Today the structure is used as an auction house. William Manchester was the village supervisor from 1820 to 1821, the time of the establishment of this church. (Courtesy of the Town of Madison Historical Society.)

The Wesleyan Chapel was organized about 1833 with a class of nine members, and meetings were held in the small chapel on the east edge of Eaton for a few years when the church in Madison was built. It was remodeled about 1871, and in 1888, the name of the church was changed to the Methodist Episcopal Church of Madison, as shown in this photograph. (Courtesy of the Town of Madison Historical Society.)

The Madison Universal Church was erected on South Street in the village of Madison in July 1828 with the Reverend Nathanial Stacy as the first pastor. This building became the American Legion and is now the home of the Town of Madison Historical Society. (Courtesy of the Town of Madison Historical Society.)

The hotel in the village of Madison was called the Madison House and was kept by F.B. Howard as of 1899. This photograph of the Madison House was taken in 1916. The hotel was located on the corner of North Street and the Cherry Valley Turnpike in the center of town. (Courtesy of the Town of Madison Historical Society.)

Here is the Madison House with the bandstand still out front. This bandstand was moved in 1931, when Route 20 was widened. This picture was taken looking west with the hotel on corner of North Street. The Madison House (called the Madison Hotel in this picture) has since been torn down. (Courtesy of the Town of Madison Historical Society.)

CLIFFORD'S OLD HOMESTEAD. CHICKEN AND STEAK DINNERS. ALL YOU CAN EAT OF THE BEST
OF EVERYTHING. PHONE 68F13, MADISON, N. Y.   B-994

This photograph reads, "Clifford's Old Homestead. Just like home. Most choice rooms. Chicken and Steak Dinners. All you can eat of the best of everything. Phone 68F13. Madison, NY." It is now known as the Old Homestead Motel, Madison Lake Estates, and Madison Lake Mobile Homes Sales and is operating at 7172 State Route 20 in Madison. (Courtesy of Helen Nower.)

Quacks Diner was originally located in the old railroad depot in Bouckville, but owner Glenn Quackenbush moved the establishment to the village of Madison. This photograph is of the original building in Madison before any additions. Glenn also drove a school bus for the Madison Central School District. (Courtesy of the Town of Madison Historical Society.)

The history of the school district begins on June 19, 1812, when the government of the State of New York passed legislation that each township of the state was to be divided into common school districts. On November 1, 1813, a meeting was held, and the town of Madison was divided into 17 districts. On December 7, 1878, the Madison Union Free School and Academy was formed. The building used was on South Street, shown here. (Courtesy of the Town of Madison Historical Society.)

On April 16, 1931, the Hinman site was chosen for site of the new central school, as it provided a panoramic view from the Cherry Valley Turnpike and would afford the children a safe hill for play. The hill and "bowl" were the result of glacial action, which formed a kettle hole. School was held in the new building for the first time on March 21, 1932. (Courtesy of the Town of Madison Historical Society.)

Nine

MADISON AND
MORAINE LAKES

Madison Lake is located in the famous hops section of Madison County, New York, on the Utica Division of the O&W Railroad, 21 miles south from Utica. Madison Lake is upwards of a mile and a half in length and a quarter-mile in width. The area was adapted for hosting private parties, society picnics, and excursions, providing beautiful shaded groves, spacious hotels, and a large lakeside pavilion.

Madison was a busy thoroughfare for east-to-west travelers and featured a hotel and resort on Madison Lake. Businessman G.W. Hinman owned much of Madison. Many visitors came from the nearby hamlet of Solsville, where the Chenango Canal and the railroad both had stations.

As the popularity of the lakes in the township of Madison grew, so did the possibility of serious accidents. Madison Lake has always been considered a dangerous lake because of its extreme depth. Between 1870 and 1946, 12 people drowned in Madison Lake—the youngest being 16 and the oldest being 60. In 1880, 17-year-old John Costello of Oran, Onondaga County, died after spending days picking hops with his sister Mary on the farm of Theodore Spencer near Madison.

Lake Moraine's principal body of water was also known as Madison Brook Reservoir in 1892. The south part of the lake covers 235 acres and was connected with the Chenango Canal. Madison Brook Reservoir was created in 1837 as a feeder reservoir of the Chenango Canal. Lake Moraine (as it is now known) has a maximum depth of 46 feet. The southern section of this lake is ringed with cottages and their associated motorboats.

Lake Moraine is known as the safer lake of the two, yet there have been 16 deaths between 1868 and 1949, with the youngest and oldest drowning victims being of an infant in 1920 and a 35-year-old man in 1947.

At Madison Lake, a quarter of a mile from the village of Madison and near the line of the Ontario & Western Railroad, are two summer hotels kept by D.W. Leland and White & Lewis, respectively. As of June 7, 1894, the first floor of the Lewis House (Madison Lake Pavilion) was completed, and the carpenters were working on the bowling alley. This photograph shows the Lewis House once completed. (Courtesy of Jim Ford.)

The Lewis House (Pavilion) had a shooting gallery located in the lower left and a saloon in the lower right. On the top floor, there was a dining room on the right side and a dance hall on the left. The lower level also had a hot dog stand and concession stand and a storage area. (Courtesy of Jim Ford.)

This c. 1900 photograph shows Pulver's merry-go-round, which was located at Madison Lake. The roadway leading to the lake from Solsville is also seen in the background. This beautiful spot has many attractions for those seeking rest and recreation and attained considerable popularity. (Courtesy of Jim Ford.)

Here is a picnic scene at Madison Lake, which was a very common event. An upright boiler ran the merry-go-round. The pavilion in the background remained at Madison Lake into the 1950s, when many students of Madison Central School and adults alike went there to roller-skate. (Courtesy of Jim Ford.)

Swimming and rowboats became popular activities at Madison Lake. The lake has a dangerous drop-off near the shore. A number of people have drowned in the lake over the years. As of October 7, 1885, Madison Lake had a new steamer, which was the first to ever sail the lake. (Courtesy of Jim Ford.)

The rush of excitement for recreation is at the shores of Madison Lake. Citizens from Waterville, Hamilton, and Knoxboro, as well as locals, have taken in hand the fitting of the grounds for picnic parties. The horses were tied away from the buggies, as seen in this picture. (Courtesy of Jim Ford.)

A large number of boarders was expected in town for the season in 1889. A man of enterprise and capital was wanted to build a good boardinghouse and a large barn at the lake. Several improvements were to be made at the lake that season. (Courtesy of Jim Ford.)

The cottages were built, enabling many families to come to Madison Lake for a week, a month, or the entire summer. Point Cottage (pictured) was a popular cottage to rent. It was constructed in the Adirondack style and had a commanding view of the lake. (Courtesy of Jim Ford.)

The formal opening of Leland Park (known as Leland House) on Madison Lake took place on Wednesday evening, July 17, 1889, with a flourish of trumpets and amid the most favorable auspices possible. The grove was splendidly illuminated, and everything showed up at its best. The Leland was one of the premier resort hotels in Central New York for many years. (Courtesy of Jim Ford.)

Here is a view of the Leland House at Madison Lake in 1910. The first floor had the public waiting room, office, bar room, ice cream room, and dancing hall; the second floor had a wing with a kitchen, pantry, and butler's pantry along with a great parlor, a large and spacious hall, sleeping rooms, and an attractive dining hall. (Courtesy of Jim Ford.)

The Chenango County Farm Bureau and Madison–Chenango County Holstein Breeder's Club cooperated to hold a big picnic at Madison Lake and an auto tour to visit a number of the best purebred dairies in Southern Madison County in 1916. This photograph is from a little later time when a picnicker drove his car to the lake. (Courtesy of Jim Ford.)

Between 30 and 40 people were injured in the collapse of a large section of the hotel veranda at Madison Lake on July 4, 1917. While a large Fourth of July dance was in progress at the Lewis, two sections of the floor of the high veranda, located on the side of the building facing the lake and next to the dance hall, gave way, throwing more than 100 screaming people 12 feet to the ground. (Courtesy of Jim Ford.)

This photograph shows the Lewis House and barns around 1915. The Lewis House Pavilion is on the right in the photograph, and the bowling alley is the one-story extension on the building. By the water, there are boats to rent and a photographer's studio. On April 15, 1875, the agents of the Madison County Sportsmen's Club put three dozen black bass into the lake. (Courtesy of Jim Ford.)

This photograph shows the "toboggan" slide at Madison Lake. The slide was set up parallel to the shore, just to the south of the Leland Hotel. Also known as the waterslide ride, this attraction proved to be very popular with guests at the lake. After climbing a set of stairs, one sat on a board and rode down the ramp on a series of rollers. (Courtesy of Jim Ford.)

The Madison Reservoir proved to be the most available for the summit of the Chenango Canal and a valuable feeder of the Erie Canal. In order to safely raise the water higher than the former high water line, a waste weir was constructed to control the height of water when it gets up as high as is safe on the embankment. (Courtesy of Madison County Historical Society.)

Although Madison Lake began to cater to campers and tourists at an earlier date than Lake Moraine, residents of the Moraine area soon began a number of business enterprises and activities. Here is a man about to enjoy a row on Madison Reservoir, also known as Lake Moraine. (Courtesy of Madison County Historical Society.)

Lake Moraine and Kimmouth Island are pictured near Hamilton around 1912. George Frank's Dance Hall and Roller Rink could be seen from the island. For many years, this was the place to go for dancing and roller-skating activities. It drew huge crowds to the events. (Courtesy of Madison County Historical Society.)

Should the dam give way to Lake Moraine from the north, the villages of Hamilton, Earlville, and Sherburne would be crushed in its mighty sweep and thousands of lives be sacrificed. Susan Summer Storke, at age 15, wrote a fitting description of this lake at sunrise. (Courtesy of Madison County Historical Society.)

Frederick Baker, age 18, drowned at Madison Reservoir on a Saturday afternoon in May 1891. With his stepfather and a young man named Pearl Abbott, he was fishing at the reservoir crossing. He was subject to fits and had evidently been seized with one and had fallen into the water, head downwards, and drowned. (Courtesy of Jim Ford.)

Shown is the Piotrow Cottage on Lake Moraine in Hamilton. While fishing for perch at Lake Moraine in May 1918, Charles Edkins, a barber, hooked what he immediately discovered to be an unusually large fish. It provided to be California brown trout weighing seven pounds and 28 inches in length. (Courtesy of Jim Ford.)

Lake Moraine, Hamilton, N.Y.

West Shore of Lake Moraine, Hamilton, N. Y.

West Shore, Lake Moraine, is located in both the towns of Madison and Hamilton. The body of Leonard White, a Madison farm hand drowned in Lake Moraine on the night of April 12, 1919, came to the surface and was recovered. The recovery was made by E.C. Butler. (Courtesy of Jim Ford.)

Pictured is Cottage Beach on Madison Reservoir. On October 22, 1891, it was reported that, in three hours fishing on Madison Reservoir, A.B. Rice caught 42 bass totalling 127 pounds. On March 12, 1896, it was reported that the water in Madison Reservoir was very low, and in consequence, the ice harvesters there were having greater difficulty than usual in securing the crop. (Courtesy of Jim Ford.)

This photograph says, "An Island in Lake Moraine, Hamilton, N.Y." There are actually four islands. During the summer of 1897, several parties from the village of Madison were taking their summer outing at Madison Reservoir. It was noted to be an easily reached and pretty spot and a place to fish. (Courtesy of Jim Ford.)

This photograph was taken looking at Lake Moraine from the north. There had been a large number of campers and picnickers at Madison Reservoir in the summer of 1899. The reservoir seemed lovelier than ever, and one reporter thought the name should be changed to Summit Lake to be an exclusive summer resort of Hamilton. (Courtesy of Jim Ford.)

The north side of Lower Lake Leland was used to harvest ice in the winter. It was state law that any person or corporation cutting ice in or upon any waters within the boundaries of the state for the purpose of removing for sale must surround the cuttings and openings made with fence or brush sufficient enough to warn all persons of such cuttings and openings. (Courtesy of Madison County Historical Society.)

This view of Lower Lake Leland looking northeast from the dam looks like a plate of glass. The Leland Pond is located in Madison County. At an elevation of 347 feet, Leland Pond is located at 42 degrees, 52 minutes North latitude, 75 degrees, 34 minutes West longitude. (Courtesy of Madison County Historical Society.)

Ten

VILLAGE OF HAMILTON

The village of Hamilton is in the Chenango Valley, just south of the headwaters of the Chenango River. The area that became the town of Hamilton (including the village of Hamilton) originally was inhabited by members of the Iroquois League. Following the American Revolution, the area was ceded to the state of New York.

In 1794, Samuel Payne moved southwest from Whitestone into the town of Hamilton to start a farm on the hill that is today's location of Colgate University. In 1795, a year after his brother moved into the town of Hamilton, Elisha Payne did so as well. He and others from Whitestone and Connecticut moved to an unsettled area just north of his brother, and that settlement grew to become today's village of Hamilton. Because of Elisha Payne's interest and ability in developing the settlement, it became known as Payne's Settlement. He built a barn, the first framed building in the village, and, in 1802, a tavern at the intersection of Broad and Lebanon Streets, taking the place of an existing tavern that had opened in 1800. This became the Park House (Hotel), which, in 1925, was replaced by the present-day Colgate Inn.

By 1800, Payne's Settlement had, in addition to log cabins, five framed buildings and a nearby sawmill. By 1806, much of the land surrounding the settlement had been cleared and replaced by orchards and farms. Salt was the accepted form of currency in the settlement. Payne's Settlement experienced a financial boom from 1800 through the War of 1812 due to extensive crop exports to Europe and to the high prices obtained for provisions in New York during the war. Serving as the trading center, the settlement naturally prospered when farmers received higher prices. In addition, the 1808 opening of the Skaneateles Turnpike, which connected the village to Western New York, probably contributed to the favorable economic climate.

There are references to Joseph Mott settling here from Bridgewater in 1821 and establishing the first drugstore. His sons Smith Mott and Joseph Addison Mott formed a mercantile business under the name of S&JA Mott until the fall of 1833. Joseph then formed a partnership with Amos Crocker for one year and then traded as a sole proprietorship until 1847.

Pictured is the Smith Block Broad Street fire that happened in the village of Hamilton. Elisha Payne made the first frame building in the town, which was a barn with hewn timbers. Squire Payne (as Elisha Payne was better known) kept the tavern in his first dwelling immediately after his arrival and settlement here. (Courtesy of Madison County Historical Society.)

Here is a snow scene from 1903 in Hamilton. There was a small frame tavern, built prior to 1802, which stood where the Park House now is. It was a small house with two rooms facing the south with a shed running back on the east. (Courtesy of Madison County Historical Society.)

Pictured is the Village Park in 1865 in Hamilton. This was a swamp area filled with dirt from the digging of the Chenango Canal through Hamilton. From 1834 to 1837, during the building of the canal, great activity in trade prevailed. More than a score of stores and shops suddenly found existence that were not, however, permanent institutions. (Courtesy of Madison County Historical Society.)

In the nine-mile swamp near North Brookfield, a large specimen of the wildcat family, a lynx, was bagged by two hunters and a pack of foxhounds on Monday, December 21, 1908. Charles Roeder (left) and Lynn Head of Madison Center pose here on the porch at the Park Hotel in Hamilton. This was the first lynx found in this section in many years. (Courtesy of Madison County Historical Society.)

This photograph, taken in April 1889, shows the "Low Down" wagon, owned by R. Hartshorn of North Syracuse. As noted on the side, this is "Parson L.D. Wagon Co." out of Earlville. The village of Earlville is most beautifully situated in the valley of the Chenango River. Four towns—Hamilton, Lebanon, Sherburne, and Smyrna—and two counties join here. (Courtesy of Madison County Historical Society.)

Payne Street is pictured in 1860. On the right is the first bank, the Hamilton Bank, which was organized on February 19, 1853, and was incorporated under the state laws on March 1, 1853. Its capital stock was $110,000, a majority of which was owned by people residing in the immediate vicinity. The building next to it reads "John C. Foote & Co." across the top. (Courtesy of Madison County Historical Society.)

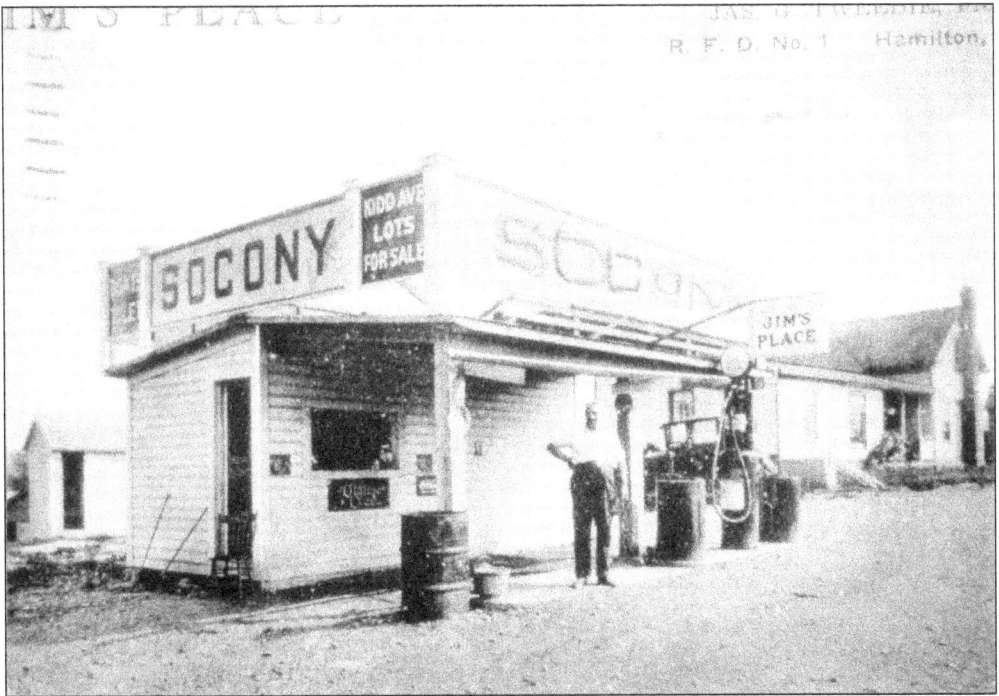

This shows SOCONY, which stands for Standard Oil Company of New York. Matthew Ewing and Hiram Everest founded it in 1866. Their product became popular for use by steam engines and internal combustion engines. It reads, "Jim's Place, Jas. G. Tweedie, R.F.D. No. 1, Hamilton." (Courtesy of Madison County Historical Society.)

Dearing & Graves built half of the brick buildings on the southwesterly side of Broad Street. Joseph Colwell and Capt. Esek Steere built the brick store, which was afterwards taken down and rebuilt by Captain Steere and became the hardware store of Foote & Gaskill. This photograph is of the village of Hamilton in 1865. (Courtesy of Madison County Historical Society.)

Although the village was the home of some of the most eminent lawyers and talented political men, the desire to promote the cause of education became the paramount idea that actuated the important movements of those days. This is a village of Hamilton streetscape seen from the park around 1865. (Courtesy of Madison County Historical Society.)

This is Hamilton High School. The old district schools of Hamilton have been merged into the Union School. In 1853, School Districts No. 1, 14, and 17 were consolidated. The district elected three trustees for a term of three years, and the trustees form a board of education and have the charge of the school. (Courtesy of Madison County Historical Society.)

From 1867, the Hamilton Female Seminary was a boarding and day school that was situated on Broad Street, near the park. The grounds, which were amply shaded in the front, surrounded and secluded in the rear by a high hedge of evergreens, and otherwise adorned by garden walks, arbors, artificial pond, and fountain, could not well be surpassed in beauty or adaptation to the school's educational purposes. (Courtesy of Madison County Historical Society.)

In 1817, six clergy and seven laymen—13 men total—met in the Hamilton with "13 dollars, 13 prayers, and 13 articles," according to *Colgate University: History and Traditions*. In that meeting, the men founded the Baptist Education Society of the State of New York, the cornerstone in the foundation of what would become Colgate University. Colgate Academy, the preparatory department, was discontinued in 1912. (Courtesy of Madison County Historical Society.)

Pictured are Colgate Gymnasium and Eaton Hall. The state chartered the Baptist Education Society in 1819, choosing Hamilton as the location for its school; one year later, the school opened. In 1823, Baptists in New York City—soap maker William Colgate among them—consolidated their seminary with the Hamilton school to form the Hamilton Literary and Theological Institution. The Colgate family connection was thus established. (Courtesy of Madison County Historical Society.)

This photograph shows the Colgate Union with a large gathering. By 1834, the institution included preparatory, collegiate, and theological departments. In 1839, the first students "not having the ministry in view" were admitted. (Courtesy of Madison County Historical Society.)

The year 1846 witnessed a name change to Madison University and, through a state charter, the right to grant degrees. In 1890, Madison University changed its name to Colgate University in recognition of the family and its gifts to the school. This photograph shows Eaton Hall at the Colgate Union. (Courtesy of Madison County Historical Society.)

The old Colgate Library became the Admissions Building. (Courtesy of Madison County Historical Society.)

Nearly all the buildings on campus are built of stone. According to the regent's report in 1870, Hamilton had 130 students, 67 of whom were pursuing a classical course; 831 volumes in its library; and a library and apparatus valued at $1,500. (Courtesy of Madison County Historical Society.)

Probably the most distinctive building on campus is the Colgate Memorial Chapel, which was built in 1918 and used for lectures, performances, concerts, and religious services. The school was founded in 1819 as a Baptist seminary and became nondenominational later. It is named for the Colgate family, who greatly contributed to the university's endowment in the 19th century. (Courtesy of Special Collections and University Archives, Colgate University Libraries.)

124

Taylor Lake was created in 1905 and named after James Morford Taylor, a member of the class of 1867. He was an instructor of mathematics from 1868 to 1918 and superintendent of buildings and grounds from the 1890s through 1920. There is a wonderful stone bridge that crosses an area of Taylor Lake at a very narrow place. (Courtesy of Madison County Historical Society.)

Written on this photograph is "Colgate versus Bouckville, at Hamilton, N.Y. Whithall Field"— baseball at its best! As early as July 1870, the baseball season opened for the Summits with a 33-30 win over the team from Hamilton; however, the Hamilton team came to Bouckville and secured an 18-6 win over the Summits in August. (Courtesy of Jim Ford.)

This is the Preservation Poolville Country Store, located in Poolville in town of Hamilton. During the period between 1830 and 1840, Poolville, with various manufactories, shops, stores, and a tavern, was wearing an air of thrift and enterprise unheard of before. The Congregational church was removed here, and a Methodist society had been organized. (Courtesy of Madison County Historical Society.)

This was the home of Frederick G. Mott on Payne Street in Hamilton around 1903. Mott first established the mercantile business on a substantial basis. His sons Smith and Addison Mott succeeded him, and on their retiring from business, it passed into the hands of a son of Smith, C.M. Mott, who perpetuates the good reputation of their house. (Courtesy of Jim Ford.)

The First Baptist Church of Hamilton was founded in 1796 and is considered the Mother Church of Colgate University. Prof. Arthur Jones, in the January 18, 1906, *Examiner*, stated that, "with the possible exception of Old First Baptist at Providence, Rhode Island, no church has had such close relations with the life of the Baptist denomination in this country as the Baptist church of Hamilton, New York." (Courtesy of Madison County Historical Society.)

St. Mary's Church, a Roman Catholic church, is located in the village of Hamilton. The church is a very uplifting place that brings a high level of spirituality and enlightenment to all who attend. This photograph shows the inside of the church. (Courtesy of Madison County Historical Society.)

Visit us at
arcadiapublishing.com

www.ingramcontent.com/pod-product-compliance
Lightning Source LLC
Chambersburg PA
CBHW050652110426
42813CB00007B/1992

* 9 7 8 1 5 3 1 6 5 0 8 2 7 *